Ana: A Memoir of Anorexia Nervosa

Syanne Centeno

The author has made every effort to ensure the accuracy of the information within this book was correct at time of publication. The author does not assume and hereby disclaims any liability to any party for any loss, damage, or disruption caused by errors or omissions, whether such errors or omissions result from accident, negligence, or any other cause. All names in this book are pseudonyms except the name of the author.
The author disclaims liability for the content of the websites identified in this book.

© 2018 Syanne Centeno All rights reserved. No portion of this book may be reproduced in any form without permission from the publisher, except as permitted by U.S. copyright law.

ISBN: 9781724064813

Cover photo by i yunmai on Unsplash
Cover design by Syanne Centeno

Table of Contents

SO IT BEGINS 10
SNEAKY LITTLE GIRL 16
SECRETS REVEALED 18
MEETING ANA 20
SPRING, 2007 21
FREAK 23
THE YEAR 2006 25
STARVING PARTNERS 30
COURAGE 34
SHRINKING GIRL 35
2.15.2007 39
SPRING 2007 39
PERFECT 41
THE FIRST VISIT 45
WATCHED 52
CHANGES 54
BAD NEWS 55
BECOMING ANA 56
RITUALS 57
YOU'RE SICK 58
THE MOVE 63
MARYLAND 65
NEW GIRL 67
FITTING IN 71
SHE'S BACK 73

FASTING	77
FASTING PT. 2	80
IT'S TIME	83
OCTOBER 27TH, 2008	86
DAY ONE	95
SURVIVAL	99
GOODBYE	104
THE ATTEMPT	107
FLOOR 5	109
ANA'S HAND	111
LIFE WITHOUT ANA	113
GET HELP	115

SYANNE CENTENO

DEDICATION

For anyone struggling with a mental illness.
You are loved and valued. Never give up.

So It Begins

Starving was my way of coping with life. If I was starving, then that meant that I did not have to face reality. I did not have to think. When you're starving, you cannot think. Every day feels like an out-of-body experience, and everything sounds like you are swimming under water. When you have Anorexia Nervosa, you aren't living… you are merely existing. You become a walking corpse of the person you once were. Your life becomes about finding ways to satisfy your disorder and nothing else really matters. You know that there is a chance that you won't wake-up the next morning, but keeping the Anorexia alive is more important than keeping yourself alive. You convince yourself that as long as you are hungry that somehow everything is okay. This was my life for 10 ½ years. My name is Syanne Centeno and I found Anorexia as an eight-year-old little girl. You could say that I accidentally stumbled upon this illness, or maybe IT actually found ME. I didn't know what Anorexia was, and had never heard of it. I actually didn't hear the term "Anorexia Nervosa" until I was 14, but had unknowingly been engaging in eating disorder behavior for years prior. Anorexia is such a complex, perplexing disorder. Trying to explain why I developed this as a child is nearly impossible. The only thing I can do is write down my experience and take you on a journey in my shoes in hopes that this will help someone somewhere understand the realities of living with an eating disorder.

Fall, September 2000

I was eight years old when I purposely skipped my first meal. I was the new girl attending a brand new school in California. I had just moved to the Golden State from the U.S. Virgin Islands. I am Puerto Rican and was born and raised in the U.S. Virgin Islands, specifically on the islands of St. Croix and St. Thomas. Before my move, people with tan or dark skin, with the exception of my mother and sister, only ever surrounded me. My mother and my older sister are also fully Puerto Rican, but their skin is white. My dad is darker like me. The only light-skinned people I was use to being around were members of my family, so I never realized that their skin color was different from mine. I did always admire my mother's beautiful green eyes though, and had always wished that I had inherited that feature from her.

It wasn't until I moved to California and attended this new school that I began to notice the difference in skin color. You would think that California has a high number of Latinos, which it does. However, I lived in Southern California, in a little town called Oak Park only 30 minutes from Hollywood, 20 minutes from Malibu, and just 10 minutes from Calabasas -- where a majority of A-list celebrities call home. The percentage of Latino's in Oak Park during that time was just 4%. Where I lived was so suburban, and so small, that locals often referred to it as "The Bubble". Every house was painted perfectly, with flawless front yards filled with bright, full green grass and a variation of colorful flowers. Children would often play outside, and mothers would stay at home while fathers worked full-time jobs. Every family was dressed exquisitely with big smiles plastered on their faces. My first impression of this place was a complete shock of its faultless nature. However, we didn't live in one of these "perfect" homes.

We moved to a small, two-bedroom apartment right past one of these neighborhoods. We didn't have a front or back yard, and the apartments were all painted a brownish color. My mother worked in an office supply store, and my dad worked for a broadcasting company. I was happy and always considered myself fortunate. I was excited about starting school in a new place that was beautiful like the movies... until I walked into my elementary school campus.

It was at that moment that I realized that my sister's skin color was actually different from mine. I wanted to disappear because I felt different. I can't quite explain it, but I immediately felt shame in the way that I looked-- something that I had never felt before.

I was one of only a handful of kids that were "brown". I instantly noticed that children who were of a different race were instantly excluded from most social groups. That is what happened to me as well.

A photo was taken of my sister and I where she was smiling and I was frowning. I don't remember who took it, but we would then receive the photo at the end of the year so that we would always remember our very first day. The irony in that situation was overwhelming because I wanted nothing more than to forget that day.

The bell rang, and it was time for class. I walked into my homeroom behind all of the other children, but they did not notice me. I don't think they wanted to notice me. They scurried off and immediately formed groups with their friends. The girls squealed as they hugged each other. They acted like they hadn't seen each other in years, even though chances were that they lived right next door to each other. I stood by myself in front of the room and quietly watched everyone chatting away. I was the only brown kid in the entire class. I wanted nothing more than to turn away and run and I might have if my teacher didn't approach me at that moment.

From head to toe, she resembled the image of a stereotypical teacher, JUST like on television shows. I know that I keep comparing this place to a movie or television show, but it IS California after all, and it was definitely a culture shock to me. No one seemed to look the way people looked like back home. No one spoke the way they did back home, either. Back home, everyone had island accents and dressed in colorful outfits. Not here. My teacher had red hair with minimal grey strands, fair skin, glasses and a beautiful smile. Her teeth were straight, unlike mine, and she wore a tan pencil skirt, a green sweater and black Mary-Jane shoes. Her shoulder-length hair was also perfectly flipped outwards. She looked down at me as her hair stayed flawlessly in place.

She introduced herself as Mrs. Denis and asked for my name. I shyly introduced myself and told her I was new. Her face lit up, and she became overly excited and said, "Let's go find you a buddy!"

I felt hopeful at this moment. As a child, I had a lot of faith in adults and I thought that they could do anything. I was positive that with her help I would find a friend. As she led me to one of the round tables, I noticed that the board was not a green chalkboard. It was actually a dry erase board. I had never seen such a big dry erase board in my life! In fact, I had never seen one that you couldn't carry around. My attention quickly shifted from the dry erase board to a round table filled with girls. They glanced up at Mrs. Denis but didn't smile.

Mrs. Denis proceeded to say, "Girls, this is Syanne. She is new and just moved here from the Virgin Islands, isn't that neat?" One of the girls stood up and coldly said, "Mrs. Denis, she can't sit here."

She avoided looking at me as if her eyes would burn if she even tried.

Mrs. Denis looked genuinely shocked by their cruelty and asked, "Why?"

The girl simply replied that I was "weird."

I knew that I was different from the other kids in class, but I had never considered myself to be "weird." Back home in the islands I had a lot of friends and was quite popular. Her spiteful comments about me were something I had never had to deal with in the past. She spoke of me as if I was not there, like she thought she was too good to acknowledge my presence.

Mrs. Denis threw her arms in the air and exclaimed, "BUT SHE NEEDS A BUDDY!"

Those words still ring in my ears as I replay these memories in my head. It was such a significant statement because I really did need a friend. Mrs. Denis and this incredibly mean child argued back and forth for a minute or two longer before Mrs. Denis decided that there was no use in debating with her.

We moved onto another table. This table had both boys and girls sitting at it and Mrs. Denis told me to take a seat there. I sat there silently and looked up at my classmates. They gave me nothing more than a quick glance and avoided making eye contact with me. I was thankful that at least they didn't protest me sitting there. The class had officially begun and Mrs. Denis was discussing the rules of the classroom. She handed out papers that would be signed by our parents and would need to be returned the next day. I shoved the papers in my binder and anxiously waited for time to pass by.

Before I knew it was recess, I was hungry, and ready to find a friendly face. Kids bumped me as they made their way out of the classroom. I watched my classmates walk with each other to the snack area, which was the same place as the lunch area. I stopped in front of my class bungalow and began to understand just how alone I was.

I curled up in front of my classroom door and opened up a bag of chips that my mother had given me as a snack in case I got hungry. As I sat there nibbling on my chips, I looked up and saw my sister walking out of class with two girls smiling. They were fair-skinned, just like her. She began looking around and I slumped down further against my classroom door so that she wouldn't see me. This was too humiliating. I began crying and spent my entire time there alone until the bell signaled the end of recess. At that moment, I decided that I wouldn't eat at lunch because I'd rather be hungry than be seen eating alone. I had never skipped a meal before and had never been hungry for more than an hour. This hunger made me feel light-headed, and I discovered that in turn that it made me feel less sad, less angry and less lonely. This was my first taste of emptiness and I instantly became addicted. This emptiness became my comfort when I was called names, isolated, and physically tormented by a bully. Hunger became my escape.

Sneaky Little Girl

I was able to get away with skipping breakfast by assuring my parents that I would eat once I got to school. My usual excuse was, "Well, I'm not hungry right now, can I just take a baggie of cereal with me?"

They would almost always allow me to. They had no suspicion of what I had been doing, and I was always an honest kid, but I had gone from being my parents' innocent daughter to a manipulative and sneaky little girl within a matter of months. I knew that lying to my parents was wrong but I couldn't risk them making me eat. Feeling "empty" was more important than being truthful.

My mom made me sandwiches for lunch and they were always either in a sandwich bag or wrapped in foil. They were the typical ham and cheese sandwiches. I would also have a bottle of water and some form of fruit or veggies like a banana or baby carrots.

I would throw them away at lunch so that I wouldn't have to eat it. I made sure that I was one of the first kids out of class so that I could make it to the lunch area before anyone else. I did this in order to quickly throw away my lunch before anyone could see. At this point, I had made friends (who were "outsiders" to most social groups), and I had to make sure that they didn't find out I was doing this, either. Once I reached the lunch area, I'd have my arms crossed, and my sandwich would be hidden somewhere in the tangles of my arms. I'd walk towards the trashcan and get as close as I could. I would then stand there for a minute and look around to make sure that none of the supervising adults were watching. When I was sure that they weren't looking, I lifted my crossed arms and the sandwich would immediately fall into the trash. I'd walk away feeling relieved that I no longer had to eat and subject myself to the awful feeling of "full." I would then walk over to our table, sit down and prepare the next excuse to explain to my friends why I wasn't eating lunch again.

Secrets Revealed

I met my friend Natasha ("Tasha" for short) in the middle of my third grade school year on the swing set of our elementary school playground. She was now labeled the "new" girl, and I was finally rid of that title. She was fair-skinned with dirty blonde hair, features that I had come to envy and desire. She was from Arizona and her parents had just gotten a divorce so her dad and her three older brothers moved to California. I never asked why she wasn't with her mom, though I had always wondered why. All I ever knew was that her mom stayed behind and she was now the only girl in her family. We not only went to school together, but we also lived in the same apartment complex. My mom became a mother figure to her, often buying her girly clothes to replace her slightly boyish garments. We would have frequent sleepovers and grew to become best friends.

We were so close that she began to notice that I always said "I already ate" at lunch, so I had to start at least pretending to eat. My new habit became to eat a couple of bites of my sandwich and say, "I'm going to save the rest for after school while I wait for my parents to pick me up."

I would then fold it back up in the foil and toss it in my backpack. She didn't think too much of it.

When I got home, I couldn't immediately throw the sandwich away because my mother was always in the kitchen cooking dinner and cleaning. My first idea was to hold it in my backpack until she left the kitchen. That never worked because I would always forget and then my backpack would develop a horrible odor. My next idea was to conceal it under my bed until I had the opportunity to throw it away. Well, I forgot that it was underneath my bed and my dog had ended up dragging it out everywhere while my mom and I went shopping.

When we had returned home, my heart dropped to the floor as I literally saw my "secrets" spread out from my room, into the living room. The odor was overwhelming. My mother looked appalled and asked, "What is this?"

"Tell her," I heard a voice say.
I ignored it as "Ana" took over and demanded that I lie. I obeyed "Ana" and responded with, "I don't know what that is." My mom bent down and picked up a piece of foil that had a-who-knows-how-old piece of food in it. She immediately recognized what it was. It was my school lunches. If it wasn't for the foil I don't think she would have been able to identify what it was. She was both enraged, and noticeably hurt. She said, "Do you realize that all of this food has been wasted?"
I shook my head no. Another lie; I did know, and I was ashamed. Every time I would hide my food I would think about my parents and how hard they work to put food on the table, and there I was throwing it away. The thing is, it was better to throw it away than have to put it in my body. While she was talking I tuned her out, all I could think about was how else I would get out of eating lunch. It didn't matter what she said because I would do it again. After that incident, she talked to a couple of my closest friends and asked them to let her know if I was not eating. I made them promise me that they would not tell her anything. They didn't understand what the big deal was about eating, so I just told them that I didn't like the food she made me. After that, they stopped asking. They vowed that my secret was safe with them and I happily continued with my sick relationship with hunger.

A couple of weeks later, Tasha came over to have one of our routine sleepovers. I didn't know when it happened, but at some point throughout her stay she had told my mom that I was still not eating and had been throwing away my food at school. This was the first friendship that Ana destroyed. I was extremely furious with Tasha. How could she do this to me? How could she try to take this away from me? I had to cut her out of my life.

I told Tasha that she was no longer allowed over because she betrayed me. Having her around made me too uncomfortable. I had to protect my illness. It would never betray me. It would never upset me. It would never hurt me. It came first.

Meeting Ana

Throughout my memoir, you will see me refer to Anorexia Nervosa as "Ana." Ana was my code name for "Anorexia." I learned about the nickname when I was a teenager through what were called "pro-Ana" websites. These were dangerous websites that encouraged eating disorder behavior. People on these forums would always talk about their disorders as if it were a real person. Worse, they talked about it as if it was their idol. An idol they worship. For example, a comment on one of these websites might say, "I was hungry but Ana told me I could only eat four crackers today." I referred to my illness this way, too. All of the time, so much so that even now as an adult, I catch myself mentioning Anorexia as a real entity. To me, Ana was real.

She was a demon who had invaded my existence. I couldn't think, I couldn't breathe, and I could not live without her permission. She was everywhere.

Spring, 2007

I first saw "Pro-Ana" websites when I was 14 years old. I had managed to become friends with one of my sister's popular friends named Danielle, who first showed me the sites. She was my first friend that was part of the "in" crowd. She was very beautiful with long, auburn colored hair and green eyes, but she was different from her popular peers.
I always wanted to be her friend because I could feel her kindness and genuine heart. I knew she would be accepting of me, but I never thought that we would actually become friends. And I definitely did not think it was ever possible that we would become best friends.

We had almost everything in common, and we became inseparable during 8th grade.
I felt incredibly important the first time that she invited me over to her house. After all, she was popular. Her house was even nicer than the usual impeccable homes that I would see! She had a huge flat-screen television and even a pool table. Her family was different from the others. They joked and interacted with one another. I thought they were incredible human beings but I wasn't used to being around such laid back adults, so I also felt slightly out of place.

We went up to her room, which was perfect by the way, and got on the computer. She turned on some music and got on the Internet to check her social media page. She talked about a couple of guys that liked her and showed me their profiles. She then shifted to showing me different social media sites of famous women that she admired. They were all very skinny and pale with blonde colored hair. At some point throughout our conversation about them, she asked, "Have you heard of Anorexia?"
I replied, "No. What is that?" She was in complete disbelief that I had never heard of it.

She then explained, "It's when you purposely don't eat. I'll show you!"

 She pulled up a web page filled with pictures of emaciated models with phrases like, "Nothing tastes as good as thin feels" and "A moment on your lips, forever on your hips." She proceeded to click on an article that said "Best Fasting Tips." She said, "This is how supermodels stay thin. See, here's a tip." She began to read, "Drink water every 30 minutes throughout the day and you will feel full. DO NOT chew gum; it will only make you feel hungrier." The word "hungrier" stood out to me. I loved feeling empty; I loved being hungry. I left her house that day curious to learn more about Anorexia Nervosa.

Once I got home, I rushed to my computer and closed the door. This was my first formal meeting with Ana. She had flirted with me throughout my childhood but now I was finally meeting her face to face. My life then quickly spiraled out of control.

Freak

When I was 12 years old I began expressing my anger and sadness through music and clothes. I wore black every day with spiked collars and spiked bracelets. I had friends who dressed similar and listened to the same music. At this point I had graduated from being "weird" to being a "freak". It was definitely an upgrade. I was always so angry during this time and had collected all of the insults that had been thrown at me by my peers and translated it into distorted eating and cutting my body.

I use to wear colorful rubber bands around my wrist. The "punk rock" kids use to say that snapping it against your arm when you were upset or stressed would calm you down. Whenever someone would call me ugly, it would send me into an internal rampage. I was particularly sensitive to being called ugly because when I was nine, a group of boys that I did not know came up to me and told me that I was ugly. They thought I should know so that I could "fix it." I was always too shy and too scared to stand up for myself. This is the memory that would always appear in my mind when someone would call me ugly.

A boy I currently liked had done just that, and it tore me up inside. He seemed to prefer fair-skinned girls and the boy I had liked before had the same preference. I never felt good enough. I started to snap the rubber band against my arm upon hearing that he thought I was "ugly and creepy." I kept replaying those words in my mind: "ugly, creepy, ugly, creepy," snapping and snapping until my arm went numb and tears were streaming down my face.

When I looked down at my arm, there were swollen red welts. Despite this, I felt the pain I was inflicting on myself was not enough.

I had been drinking a can of soda and had taken the metal cap off. I remembered that some of the other kids would cut themselves to rid themselves of any ill feelings. They always said that it actually worked. I had always wondered if this would work for me.

I hesitantly began pressing the metal cap against my arm as hard as I could. My heart was racing and my mind was in over drive. A trickle of blood had seeped out as I slowly dragged the metal across my arm. It didn't hurt and I actually thought that it felt good. When I saw the blood my heart slowed down and my mind did as well. *So, this is why they do it*, I thought.

 I felt calm, and was able to continue on with my day without having to face the fact that I was incredibly depressed. Cutting became something that quickly became out of my control. By the time a month had passed, I was cutting myself at least three times a day. I wrote about it in my diary on March 15, 2004, four days before my 12th birthday.
"I found something that calms me down." I wrote excitedly. "I've been doing it for like four weeks." I drew a smiley face at the end of that sentence, and I felt so proud of my discovery. "I've been cutting my arms. I know it sounds bad, but I swear it's not." I proceeded to draw a photo of my arm with details of the cuts. "I tried to write Hate with the blade in my arm, but it didn't work. It's so dull so I have to press hard." I drew a picture of a razor and a knife.

As my self-mutilation evolved, I used different types of sharp objects to cut my arms. I used bottle caps from cans, and when I could, I would steal razor blades from my parents that would go inside of their shaving razors. They never noticed anything was missing because I'd take one and make it last for a month at a time. And because I wore long sleeves to cover the injuries, they never saw what I had been doing. It took two years for anyone to realize that I was mutilating my body, and by this time it had become an addiction that I couldn't quit.

The Year 2006

I was a very brilliant child and had always been on the honor roll. Of course, that all changed as I sunk deeper into my fixation with hunger and self-injury.
I did not care about my body or my health and I certainly had no concern for my schoolwork. All I could think about throughout the day was skipping meals and my next opportunity to obsessively cut my arms and most importantly, how to keep people from finding out and stopping me. The thoughts were repetitive and made it exhausting to even try to pay attention. Eventually, my grades dropped to a 1.7 GPA in my 8th grade year. Some of my teachers became concerned, especially my 8th grade math teacher.
Her name was Mrs. Koder and I thought that she resembled a hippie from the early 70's. She had small, round glasses and very long, faded brown hair. She was a very kind woman. Students often took advantage of her kindness and would misbehave because they knew that they would face no consequences for their actions. I really liked her but I hated math. It was my worst subject but she always tried her best to make it interesting.

In the middle of the year, we were assigned a project that taught us how to use fractions, percentages, and pie charts. We had to pick four musicians of our choice and ask our peers who their favorite was and make a mathematical chart out of the results. I chose Good Charlotte, Simple Plan, Taking Back Sunday and Nirvana to be the choices in my project. I was thrilled about this assignment because it incorporated music and it gave me the opportunity to see what my peers favorite ones were out of the four. I wanted to know because then I could attempt to fit in by pretending that whatever their favorite was was my favorite too.
The day that we began the project I was wearing a black hoodie with long sleeves with an image of a skull and roses on the back. The hoodie was loose on me due to my low weight

especially around the arms. As I wrote, my sleeve slid down to the middle of my arm and exposed my scars and newer lacerations. I had a dozen cuts on my arm from the day before. I knew the number of cuts since I always counted each slice I made.

My math teacher had just walked by as the sleeve slid down and her mouth fell open as she noticed the amount of gashes that I had on such a small area.

I looked up and saw the unsettled look on her face as she continued to stare even after she had already passed my desk. I quickly pulled down my sleeve and smiled at her. I thought that maybe smiling would assure her that I was fine and would stop her from notifying my parents or my guidance counselor. I quickly found out that she wouldn't be swayed by my cunning grin when she didn't smile back. She sat down at her desk and faced away from me. After a minute of sitting in her chair with a blank look on her face, she picked up the phone and proceeded to speak to someone as she glanced over at me.

I wasn't going to get away with this one. After a couple of minutes, she hung up and spent the rest of the class sitting at her desk. I honestly thought that I was off the hook because I wasn't called to the office right away. But about an hour into my next class, I was told that I needed to go to the office to see the guidance counselor.

I nervously entered the administrative building and was told to have a seat. A few moments later the guidance counselor, Miss Abram, called me into her office. Even though she had been my counselor for two years prior I don't think I had formally met her before. She was a thin, middle-aged woman with glasses and a big smile. She had a high-pitched voice and sounded just like a Disney princess. She was unusually cheerful, and her upbeat personality annoyed me. There's just no way that someone is that happy and if she was, she shouldn't be. I mean, how could she be?

She proceeded to introduce herself and attempted to pronounce my name. I sighed and enunciated it for her, annoyed that she couldn't say it correctly. That's a beautiful

name," she said. I was so used to hearing that compliment that I just robotically replied, "Thank you."
She smiled, and began shuffling through her notes.

"Syanne, Mrs. Koder had some concerns after seeing some cuts on your arm. Would you mind showing me?" she asked.
I immediately answered with a lie, "Cuts? What cuts? Oh, you mean the ones that my dog gave me? We play rough sometimes, it's no big deal."
A worried look seemed to develop on Miss Abram's face as I said this. I could instantly tell that this lie wasn't going to work. She ignored my response and said, "Syanne, are you hurting yourself?"

I became silent as I searched for another lie to make my last statement seem more truthful.
"May I please see your arm?" She asked again.
I couldn't seem to be able to respond quickly enough. It was no use. I lifted my sleeve and hesitantly extended my arm and her eyes grew. Due to her obvious astonishment, I told her that it wasn't as bad as it looked. She asked me why I would hurt myself in this way. I told her that I wasn't sure -- that it just made me feel better.
"Feel better about what?" She asked. I ignored her question.
"Are you going to tell my parents?" I asked fearfully.
"I promise I won't do it again. I don't have to do it. I can easily stop. Just please don't tell my parents."
This, of course, was another one of my efforts to protect my habit. She paused for a moment, and then pulled out a pen and a new sheet of notepaper.
"I'll make you a contract. You need to come in and see me on a weekly basis and allow me to look at your arms. If you don't have any fresh injuries then I won't call your parents but you have to follow the contract, okay?"

I nodded my head, smiled and agreed as she wrote up a document stating that I would not cut myself and would follow-up with her on a weekly basis. I proceeded to sign this "document" and I thanked her for keeping this matter private. I left her office feeling relieved that my parents would not be notified. I didn't really intend on stopping. The worse thing she could have done in that incident was trusting me. I wasn't going to follow some stupid piece of paper with no real meaning. She was only going to be checking my arms. Not anywhere else. What this meant was that any future self-mutilation would have to be done on my thighs. She couldn't check me there.

After a few weeks of visiting with her, I had falsely earned her trust back and she stopped checking my arms for cuts. I would only go in from time to time for an update on my progress. I had fed her mind with my made-up world of self-acceptance and love -- and she ate every single word of it. I had also done enough extra credit (which was copied from someone else's papers, by the way) to graduate from 8th grade, and had cheated my way to a higher GPA. After a few months, I stopped seeing her because she mistakenly believed that I was now "on my way to success."
It wasn't long before I returned to cutting my arms instead of my thighs. This time, I was confident that I could hide my cuts better from everyone. This time, I wouldn't get caught.

I Cut Myself
I was watching television with my mother in her room one day and had been holding the remote control up to change the channel. My sleeve had fallen down past my wrist and my cuts became exposed. I guess she noticed because a few minutes later she asked me what happened to my arms. I very casually told her that I fell. Lying became such a natural response to most conversations. But that wasn't a very good lie. I had run out of good excuses.
The pain on my mother's face upon hearing my response was easy to read. Denial wasn't going to work this time and I didn't have the energy to think since I had skipped breakfast, lunch and threw away most of my dinner. I exploded and the truth spilled out.
I began to try to explain. "I cut myself, mom. I don't know why… I'm just really sad all the time, and angry. And I hate myself."
This was the first time that I had ever been straightforward with her about my emotions and my problems.
"Why do you hate yourself?" she asked, her voice shaking.
 I paused for a moment before saying, "I don't know; because I'm ugly; because boys don't like me, because people think, I'm a freak, because I'm not white."
I felt like crying. I really did hate myself. I hated myself more than I hated anything else in the world.
My mom sighed in deeply before replying, "You need to stop caring about what people think, and I've told you this before. You are not ugly, you are not a freak and boys are stupid at this age."
I was irritated that she didn't comprehend the complexity of my situation. Her simple answer was not going to sway my opinion of myself. I rolled my eyes and became angry.
"You're just saying that. You don't understand. I HATE MYSELF. Don't you get it? I hate everything. I'm not just saying that, I mean it. If I were white things would be different, but I'm stuck like this forever." Acceptance of my race and appearance was something that I struggled with.

I stormed out of her bedroom and went to my room and closed the door. I could hear her weeping in the other room. I felt horrible for making her cry but a part of me wanted her to know what I was doing because secretly, I did want help. Even though I acted like I wanted to continue cutting myself, deep down I wanted nothing more than to just stop. But I couldn't just stop.

As guilty as I felt for making my mom upset, I reluctantly reached down under my bed and pulled out my razor and sliced my skin open until my entire arm became too sore to move. This was both a punishment for hurting my mom and a sort of "self-medication" to soothe myself from the overwhelming shame that I felt. I counted each slash that I made until there was no more room horizontally or vertically for another slice. I laid on my bed, bleeding and dazed as I drifted off to sleep with a razor in hand.

Starving Partners

When I entered 9th grade, I rekindled an old friendship with a close friend from elementary school. Her name was Abigail, Abby for short. She was tall with long, dark blonde hair and brown eyes. She was absolutely beautiful and actually looked entirely different from what I had remembered. When we were kids she had somewhat crooked teeth. She was short, and had baby fat. Sometimes the other kids would even comment that she was "chubby." Now, she was thinner than the average girl in school, had braces and grew to be a gorgeous girl.

Though we had attended the same school for years we somehow stopped being friends and I hardly ever saw her around. I don't know what happened but after 4th grade we just stopped talking. I assumed that it was because I became beneath her in the social hierarchy and we naturally grew apart. She was in my P.E class, which was our first class together since we were little kids. We both dreaded physical exercise and began talking again as we both stood on the sidelines during any strenuous physical activities. We soon found out that we still had everything in common, even after five years of no communication. She quickly grew to become one of my best friends again.

A couple of months into the year, I remembered that Abby was friends with Danielle, the friend who had shown me the pro-Ana websites. I started to wonder if her thin frame was a result of skipping meals or if she was really that naturally slim.
Though Danielle had not directly told me that she was skipping meals, I always knew it and I had a feeling that Abby was doing it, too.
I don't know what made me feel inclined to tell her about my eating problems but one day I felt like I just had to tell her. Maybe it was because I was tired of feeling alone in this or maybe I just wanted to brag about my self-control like I do on pro-Ana websites. It was probably the latter -- because there was just no way that Abby was genetically that skinny. During a sunny day in P.E class I was feeling sick from having skipped breakfast and lunch and she noticed that I was very sluggish. She asked me if I was okay and I responded with, "Abby, have you ever not eaten on purpose?"
She didn't seem at all bothered by my question.
She simply responded with, "Yes, why?"
I said, "Well, because I skip meals every day."
She answered nonchalantly, "I do, too. Breakfast, lunch and even dinner sometimes."

As strange as this sounds, I was so happy to hear her say this. I needed someone to be able to talk to about this that understands the struggle of it all.

I curiously asked her, "How much do you weigh?"

She hesitantly replied with, "One hundred nine pounds, what about you?"

I felt good that I weighed less than her and proudly declared, "I am ninety-five pounds right now, and my goal is to lose ten pounds. I've lost thirteen pounds since I began fasting."

"Wow, you are ninety-five pounds?" she said as she wrinkled up her nose.

She said this as if she didn't believe me. I began to wonder, do I not look skinny enough to be ninety-five pounds? Am I still chunky?

"Yes, I am ninety-five pounds!" I said defensively.

"Oh. Okay. You're shorter than me so we're probably about the same. I'm 5'7". How tall are you?"

I felt like she was envious of my lower weight and I was reluctant to answer.

"Umm...I'm 5'4" but the ideal weight for someone my height is supposed to be one hundred-twenty pounds, so I am still very underweight." I sharply replied.

"I'm still very underweight, too." She answered abruptly.

I looked down and glared at the ground.

"Well, what do you do to lose weight?" I asked.

"I literally just don't eat a lot." She answered confidently.

"Me neither. Have you ever been on any of the pro-Ana websites?" I inquired.

"A few times, why?" she asked curiously.

"Well, because I get a lot of my fasting tips and 'thinspirations' from those pages." I paused. "Did you know that Danielle goes on those websites?"

"Are you serious?" She asked surprised. "Did she tell you that?"

"Well, not directly. But one day we were over at her house, and she pulled up the website and was looking at fasting tips. She even told me that the 'thinspo' girls were her idols." I stopped for a moment. "But don't tell her I told you that because she didn't downright say that she was starving herself. I just figured that she was because of what she said."
"I had no idea. I mean she's skinny and everything, but she also has big boobs, so I thought that she was just lucky." She said.
"Yeah, well she's lucky she's able to get skinny and keep her boobs. I wish I could do that." I covetously replied.
From that day on we proceeded to indulge in our obsession with "Ana" and our bodies together. We were no longer the typical friends that would sit around and talk about boys all day. Instead, we talked about our new lover, Ana. We would mostly exchange fasting tips and discuss our goal weights. Sometimes we would talk about recovery but we were starving partners, not recovery buddies.

Courage

Abby and I had a couple of songs that we often quoted. The songs were about Anorexia, and our favorite one was called "Courage" by Super chick. When we were together, we would sing the lyrics in unison. The lyrics spoke about having to hide our illnesses and about how one day we would feel good enough about ourselves not to have to find validation through Ana. Though this was what we said we ultimately wanted, we did little to reach that goal because in reality, we couldn't care less about recovery. We didn't have the courage to free ourselves of Ana, we were more concerned with reaching goal weights and our competitive nature interfered with finding wellness.

I always felt like if I ever tried to stop she would reach her goal weight and I never would. That was not okay with me. I felt like reaching my goal weight was more important than staying healthy and alive. I also didn't know what it felt like to be well or to be happy. I was used to sadness and that became my normal. I was afraid of recovery and I was terrified of letting Ana go. "She" became all I knew and at the end of the day, "she" knew how to make me feel better than anything or anyone else. I could no longer hear God's voice pleading with me to seek Him; all I could hear was the whisper from Ana telling me that she was the only thing that mattered. I don't think that people realized just how sick I would become in the coming years.

Shrinking Girl

When I was 14 ½ years old, I became more and more serious about my fasting. I began documenting my caloric intake in a notebook and even began exercising aggressively.

My obsession with hunger and my appearance was no longer a secret and my parents knew that I was now a full-blown, out of control Anorexic. Even though they didn't immediately admit that they knew, I was no longer hiding it and would blatantly talk about how I needed to be skinnier in front of everyone. I did not care if anyone knew anymore and in some ways, I wanted people to know. My eating disorder made me feel superior, like somehow I was secretly above everyone else because I did not have to eat. As if I was superhuman. I could control myself from stuffing my face unlike the majority of society. *I'm better than them, see. I was the amazing shrinking girl. Watch as I get smaller and smaller!*

I felt like my disease was an asset, and really believed that starving was the only thing that I was good at. I had developed such a fascination with models and the entire modeling industry that my only desire in life was to become society's perfect, generic image of beauty. I decided to enter a modeling contest that was being hosted by my favorite teen magazine. They claimed that they were looking for girls ages 13-17 of "all backgrounds" and that "height and size didn't matter." I felt like this could be my chance to be happy, and I immediately begun begging my mother to pay the $25 entrance fee for me. After days of pleading with my mother, she finally gave in and gave me the money to enter the competition.

The guidelines stated that they needed a headshot, and a full body shot with minimal makeup. I placed my camera on a timer and stood perfectly still in front of the lens with a blank look on my face. I had researched the top modeling agencies in the world and always noticed that their models had a haunting, blank expression in their Polaroids. I tried to imitate them and thought that I had done a perfect job. I sent the photos in feeling hopeful that I could at least place in their top 12. If I placed in their top 12, then maybe I was prettier than I thought I was. Maybe I was skinny, and maybe I was more valuable than I had thought all of these years.

The next three weeks I was high on excitement as I daydreamed about the possibility of me being placed in the top 12. If you made the list, the magazine would fly you to Florida for an all-expenses paid, weeklong trip to a photo-shoot that would be in their magazine. The winner would receive a $100,000 modeling contract with one of the world's leading modeling agencies and they would be on the cover of their magazine's summer issue. I wanted nothing more than to be the girl that was good enough to be on their cover.

I compulsively frequented the magazine's website throughout the day to compare myself to past winners. I would hold a mirror up to the side of the computer as I tried to see if there was any resemblance between them and myself. I would convince myself that our eyes were kind of the same or that we had similar face shapes -- so I must stand a chance in making it into the finals. I became so overwhelmingly fixated on the competition that I even printed out photos of the past winners and taped them on to the headboard of my daybed. I thought maybe if I stared at them when I fell asleep that I'd magically turn into one of them when I'd wake up.

I even broke my fasts several times during those three weeks because I felt that maybe, just maybe I wouldn't need Ana anymore soon. If I were happy, I wouldn't need hunger to soothe me anymore. But of course, it didn't happen that way.

Friday, the day before the results were to be revealed, I didn't sleep. Instead, I spent the entire night repeating the words, "Please God, put me in the top 12. Please God, put me in the top 12. Please God…" I told myself that if I said it hundreds of times, my wish would become a priority on the top of God's checklist. I really believed this.

At around 7 a.m. the following morning, I jumped out of bed and immediately turned on my computer. *The results should be on their website now.* My stomach was in knots as I typed in the magazine website URL in my search bar. When I pressed enter, the page would instantly appear on my screen with the top 12. Before I proceeded, I said one more prayer, took a deep breath, closed my eyes tightly and pressed the enter key. I cracked my eyes slightly open and saw that the page had come up. I closed them again and I said, "This will either make me, or break me." I opened my eyes to look for my photo and name. I didn't see it. My eyes frantically danced around the screen a second time. I still didn't see myself. *"Maybe I missed it,"* I thought as I desperately searched through the list for the third time.

Nope. Nothing. I didn't make the top 12, the top 20, the top 50, or even the top 100.

I was a no one. I failed. But what else was new, right?

"Really, did you expect that you were good enough?" whispered Ana.

I stared at the girls who would be advancing in the competition as tears began forming in my eyes. *No, I'm not good enough.* I was initially sad, but the more I stared at the finalists, the more my rage overpowered my sadness. "Bitches," I quietly hissed. I suddenly reached out and punched my computer screen.

I looked over to see if I had woken up my older sister but luckily she was in a deep sleep.

"Bitches," I quietly muttered to myself again. Although it seemed that I was angry with them, I was not. My reaction was just a reflection of how badly I felt about myself.
I left my computer, and approached my bed. I ripped down the photo I had from the previous top 12, reached under my bed and picked up my journal. My journal had a pouch where little things could be kept. In this pouch was a razor and pictures of emaciated models. I grasped for the razor and forcefully pushed it against my arm as I sobbed. Three slashes ended up being all I needed to help me stop crying because I had made them much deeper than usual. I opened up my journal again and placed the razor back in its' secret pocket. I then picked up a pen and began writing my thoughts.

2.15.2007

If you haven't guessed it already, I didn't make it into the final contest. Of course, I didn't...I should have known. I'm fat, short lard. I wish that I were different. I'm a poor excuse of a person. P.S. I'M A FATASS. Tomorrow I won't eat anything."

And I didn't touch food for the next few days. I needed something to help me be loyal to my eating disorder when I was feeling a lack of self-control so I turned to my favorite pro-Ana website. On this website was a new post that contained a list called the "Thin Commandments". I instantly fell in love with this list, and frantically wrote it in my journal so that I could easily access it when I needed motivation to continue starving.

Spring 2007

In March 2007, I received laxatives as a birthday gift from my "starving partner," Abby.
"If you ever have too much liquid in a day, this will get rid of a lot of it! It will help you weigh less," she said.
 I had stopped eating solid food most days and would only drink beverages that were low in calories. The laxatives became a lifesaver for when I would surpass my caloric restrictions through liquid consumption. I first started drinking only orange juice throughout the day because I remembered how the last two times that I had fainted, my mom gave me orange juice and I would instantly feel better. She told me that it helped me feel better because it would raise my blood sugar to a normal level. This was one way that I could keep food out of my body without fainting, but since my stomach was empty it would give me heartburn and I'd end up feeling sick. Plus, it had too much sugar, and as we all know--sugar turns into fat.

I searched on the Internet for low calorie, low-fat drinks and I found soymilk. I know that skim milk may have been better, but I just couldn't get it down. It was disgusting.
I drank chocolate soymilk because it tasted better than the white soymilk. Since it was chocolate, it was a tad bit higher in calories than its' plain counterpart so I'd have to reduce my intake to just 2-3 cups a day. I was very careful not to fill the cup all the way to the brim because I hated anything being full, even dishware. Soymilk helped reduce the number of fainting spells that I would get from fasting.

I would normally pass out after taking a shower. I took long, warm showers and standing for as long as I did in a humid environment would physically drain me. My long showers were spent pinching different parts of my body to see how much skin and fat I could fit in between two fingers. I didn't care how dizzy I was getting; I had to make sure that I measured each part of my body perfectly. I'd grab my skin so hard that I often left red marks all over my body.
"Ew." I'd say to myself. "This is pathetic. Disgusting."
I always hated my legs and my stomach the most. I considered myself to be bottom heavy and I blamed that on my Latin roots. Once I'd get out of the shower, I would weigh myself ten times in a row (I was sure to count) to make sure that the scale was accurate. The scale, by the way, was another birthday gift from my "starving partner" Abby.
It was April 2007, I now weighed ninety-five pound, and I lost a total of sixteen pounds since October and wanted to lose ten more. Most days I'd go slightly over my 300-calorie restriction, which would result in either strenuous exercise for an hour or more use of laxatives. I usually chose the laxatives because I didn't have the energy to burn off the calories through exercise. I didn't really like laxatives but I had to do them. It was the only way that I could get rid of liquid weight. There was just no way that I was going to keep that crap in my body.

Perfect

I made a new friend in geography class, who I would soon find out was also an eating disorder victim. Her name was Tahlia. Here's the thing about her -- she was perfect. I mean, if I ever saw perfect -- she was it. She had long, dark black hair with pale porcelain skin and bright blue eyes. Her bones were beautiful as they protruded through her glistening, white skin.
We became friends when the teacher assigned her seat to be next to mine. She was a friend of Danielle's, just like Abby and I, so we immediately clicked since we had mutual friends. My teacher was a pushover so we literally did nothing but talk for the full hour and 45 minutes of class. We were gossiping one morning, and Tahlia was making gestures with her hands to describe a girl she didn't like. This was when I noticed that one of her knuckles appeared to be bleeding. The more I stared at her hands as she spoke, the more I noticed that there were surrounding scars and scabs. I had read on a website that bulimics often have scars on their hands, specifically on their fingers and knuckles. I wanted her to know that I knew what she was. She was a bulimic.
"Whoa, what happened to your hands?" I asked.
"Nothing, I fell." She answered defensively.
I instantly recognized this lie. It was one of my favorite lies for hiding my cutting. I knew she wasn't telling the truth.
"You fell on your knuckles?" I asked her suspiciously.
"Yes," She quickly replied.
I went ahead and asked her a more difficult question.
"How are you so skinny?" She became silent. She was starting to figure out that I was onto something.
I continued, "I wish I could be skinny like you."
She rolled her eyes and said, "Oh, please. I'm not skinny."
I paused. "You know, I read online that sometimes people who make themselves throw-up get cuts and scars on their hands. I've always wondered why."
She sighed in deeply before answering, "Well, from biting down."

"Why do they bite down?" I questioned.
She plainly said, "So that no one will hear them throwing up."
"Oh," I replied.
 She basically just admitted that she was bulimic. If she weren't, how would she even know that? So I subtly let her know that I was a fellow eating disorder worshipper too.
"I skip meals but I could never make myself throw up. I'm not brave enough for that. I tried it once and just couldn't do it. Sometimes, I wish I could, though."
"It's really easy!" She said confidently. "I mean if you're just starting out it takes forever to actually throw up. You could literally sit there for an hour trying to make yourself puke. It's hard the first time for most people. It's easier to use the back of a toothbrush to trigger your gag reflex for beginners. Once you get the hang of it, you can throw up right away with just a finger or two."
She lifted her hand up to show me her knuckles and said, "I'm bleeding a little bit right now because I threw up before class."
I looked over her small, fragile frame again.

I always thought that bulimics were either normal or average weight. But she was thinner than I was, even though she binges and purges. I didn't understand how this was possible. I used laxatives, which I always heard was also a form of purging so why was I not as skinny as her?
I decided that it was probably genetics. She was white and I was Hispanic. Statistically, Hispanics have a more difficult time losing weight and are often overweight. I could not stand being Hispanic. I felt like I had more disadvantages in life because of my race and having a hard time losing weight was the worst disadvantage out of all of them.
"I hate being Latina..." I said with a sigh.
"I didn't even think you were Latina you act so white!" she said, shocked. I took this as a form of a compliment. I smiled and said, "Thank you! I just wish my genetic make-up were Caucasian. If I were white, I wouldn't have such a hard time losing weight. I could be skinny like you."

She laughed and said, "First of all, I'm not skinny yet. Secondly, my mom is huge, so I actually have to work extra hard to get skinny."

"*She must have a secret, then.*" I thought to myself. I looked at her confused.

"Well, can you give me a tip on how I could lose more weight?"

She grinned, looked around and said, "I'll do something better…"

She reached into her pocket and pulled out a dark red capsule. "These were my mom's. She stopped using them because they made her feel sick. She has two bottles sitting in her medicine cabinet so I poured half of one bottle into a zip lock baggie. Since she doesn't take them anymore, she hasn't noticed that anything is missing. I keep 2 or 3 pills in my pocket to take during the day. You can have these, I have more at home."

I glanced around to make sure no one was looking, reached out my hand and she dropped all three capsules in my hand. I quickly closed my hand and shoved the pills into my front pocket.

"So, how does it work?" I asked, thrilled about my new "miracle" pills.

"You can take one during breakfast, lunch and dinner. Technically, you're supposed to eat when you take diet pills because they can make you feel sick on an empty stomach. You also have to drink them with a full glass of water. I figured out that you don't have to eat as long as you drink water all day," She replied.

"So, as long as I drink water all day I won't feel sick or have any problems?" I asked.

I always heard horror stories about diet pills, which is why I never went looking for them. The Ana girls online always said to be wary of them because they can kill you before you ever reach your ultimate goal weight. Dying before reaching your goal weight would be humiliating. But if Tahlia was taking them without any problems and she was skinnier than me, then I shouldn't have any problems either.

"You'll feel a little bit weird, but that's okay. You may sweat and get a little warm, and your heart might start racing, but that's just your body working to get rid of all of the fat and calories. Don't worry about it."

"So...I can take one now?" I inquired excitedly.

"Go for it!" She responded brightly. I reached back into my pocket and pulled out one red pill. I looked at it in my hand under my desk and searched around the room once more before popping it into my mouth. I took a big gulp of water from my water bottle, sat back and waited to become perfect. A couple of hours later while I was in science class, I began to feel hot.

"Holy crap, it's getting hot in here!" I thought to myself.

She said I would get a "little bit warm," but it literally felt like I was sitting in front of a blazing fire.

The next thing I knew my palms were sweating profusely, I could hear my heart in my ears, and I could also feel it beating in my throat. I also felt an incredible surge of energy. I pulled out my cell phone under my table so that my teacher wouldn't see.

I was texting Tahlia. I asked her to meet me in the bathroom ASAP.

I raised my hand and asked the teacher if I could use the restroom.

As soon as she said yes, I jumped up, grabbed the bathroom pass and sprinted out of class. When I got to the bathroom, Tahlia wasn't there yet. I paced back and forth for three minutes until she finally arrived.
"Dude, is this normal? I feel like my heart is going to push through my chest!" I said, worried that I was having a heart attack or something. I turned on one of the bathroom faucets and began running cool water on top of my sweaty hands.
"It's normal, I told you that your heart might feel like it's racing." She answered, reassuringly.
"I just didn't expect it to feel like this. This feels terrible" I whined.
"It'll get better! I promise! Pretty soon, you'll see the weight fall off. You just have to push through it! Don't give up," she encouraged.
"I'll never give up on being skinny," I answered back.
 I went back to class, sat down, and drifted into a daydream. I dreamt about how I'd soon be skinny like Tahlia. I dreamt about being the world's top model. But to be the best I had to be the thinnest and I was desperate enough to do anything I could to get there.

The First Visit

I became too weak and too sick from the combination of laxatives, diet pills and starvation that I had to make a surprise visit to the emergency room. It was my first ever visit to the E.R and I was scared. I had tried to avoid ever going to the doctor or the hospital but my parents had no choice but to take me after I suffered a fainting spell.

I was still very weak even a couple of hours after passing out and that was not normal for me. I even tried drinking orange juice and that still didn't help me feel better. In addition to that, I was having sharp stabbing pains in my stomach, and was clearly dehydrated.

I felt terribly ill so I didn't even try to convince my parents that I didn't need to go. I knew that this was potentially an emergency. If I didn't go then, I might never reach my goal weight. I just had to be cautious about what I told the doctor so that he doesn't interfere with my fasting.

Once we got there I was pulled into the back for a short assessment. My mother stayed in the lobby. They took my temperature, my blood pressure and my weight.

"Wow, you're a skinny little thing," the nurse said. The scale said 91 lbs. I felt exhilarated by both my weight, and the nurse's compliment. I tried not to show my excitement because then they might suspect that I was Anorexic.

I looked at her and said, "Yeah, I know. I hate it." I was a master manipulator, an expert in the field of deception. Obviously, I didn't hate it.

She smiled at me and said, "Well, enjoy it now because once you get older, life catches up to you." She was kind of chubby, and short. I was sure that if I didn't starve myself, I would probably end up looking like her. And there was nothing worse than being a fat person. I will die before I let life "catch up" to me.

After taking my vitals and weight, I sat down with her as she typed on a computer.

"What made you visit the hospital today?" she asked.

I think I have the flu," I responded. "I've been having diarrhea and haven't really been eating as much because everything I eat is making me have to use the restroom. I'm nauseous, too. I had such bad diarrhea that I fainted!" That's not really what happened.

"Are you vomiting?"

"No, just diarrhea" I answered.

She nodded and said, "Okay, you're probably dehydrated... how long have you been sick?"
I paused for a moment. I needed to think of a timeline that wasn't too long or too short.
"Well, today will be the third day," I answered.
"Okay, I'm going to put this bracelet on you and there will be a bed available shortly. You can have a seat back in the lobby," She kindly said.
I sat and waited in the lobby as I clenched my stomach. It felt like I had been waiting for almost an hour before I was called back. I was instructed to lie in the hospital bed and was told that the doctor would be in shortly. I rehearsed everything in my mind that I had told the nurse so that I wouldn't forget. When the doctor came in, he proceeded to ask me the same questions that the in-the-front-nurse asked.
"Well, from what it sounds like, you likely just have a viral infection, like the flu." He said.
I nodded my head and answered, "Yes that's probably what it is because some of my friends were sick recently, too." That was a lie.
"Are you having any other symptoms besides the nausea after eating and the diarrhea?" he asked.
"No." I lied again. I couldn't let him perform any tests that could possibly reveal my secret to him.
"Okay, good. I would like for you to give us a urine sample to be sure that nothing else is going on." I frowned.
"Why? I don't have to pee," I stated sharply.
"We only need a little bit. We are going to go ahead and give you some IV fluids to help rehydrate your body, and that will help you provide us with a sample. We will also be getting some vials of blood for testing of any other possible causes to your symptoms."
He asked me to extend my arm out so that the nurse could put in the IV and obtain a blood sample.
 I crossed my arms and said, "No... I hate needles..."

My mom was clearly annoyed by my childish behavior that she just said, "It'll be very quick. Just let them do it and we'll be able to leave soon."

I slowly extended my arm out and closed my eyes as the nurse pierced my vein with the needle. I was worried about the blood test but what could I do? Refusing the test would only make me look more suspicious. They gathered a couple of vials of blood, and then placed me on an IV bag.

My heart started racing at the thought of all of this fluid going inside of my body.

I was probably going to bloat somehow.

"You should be able to provide a urine sample in no time. When you're ready, just let us know and we'll disconnect you from the IV bag," the nurse said. They then both left the room. I lay there nervously for the first 15 minutes. And then, I began to feel better. I didn't feel as weak or as faint as I did when I first walked in. The stomach pains were still there but they didn't hurt nearly as bad as they did an hour before. About another 15 minutes later, I had the urgent need to pee.

"*Oh no…*" I thought to myself. I tried to hold it in. I didn't want any tests. My anorexic friends always said to avoid tests as much as I can. They told me that even urine tests could show if you're not eating. I flexed and I flexed doing my best to hold it in but it became unbearable. I had to relieve myself. I called for the nurse, she disconnected my IV and I made my way to the restroom. She handed me a little plastic cup and 2 wipes.

"Wipe first, and then urinate half way through your stream into the cup."

I nodded and said, "Okay."

I did something completely different, of course. Upon entering the restroom, I began pacing around. Partly because I really had to pee and partly because I had to figure out a way to make it look like I peed. I glanced at the sink and a crafty idea soon came to my mind.

I will fill the cup with water, and a little bit of pee.

I sat on the toilet, filled the cup about a third of the way with urine, and filled the rest with just a little bit of warm water. *HA, this should work perfectly!*
I figured that I had enough urine in the cup for it to look legit, and enough water to dilute my urine sufficiently for any testing done to come back normal. I was smart and incredibly manipulative. I even made sure that the water was hot enough for the cup to feel warm on the outside, as if it were a genuine urine sample. I walked out of the restroom with a smirk, handed the urine sample to the nurse and said, "Thank you!" as I happily walked back to my room.
I thought that I was so clever. I thought that I had tricked them into believing that it was nothing more than a stomach bug. I couldn't be more pleased with myself at that moment and neither could Ana.
As I waited for the doctor to return, I closed my eyes and began drifting into a sleep. I was completely relaxed, and knew that the testing would come back normal. The doctor returned with a nurse who checked my IV bag. It was almost empty.
"I can go home soon!" I thought.
"Jamie, go ahead and put another IV bag on there," the doctor ordered.
"Wait, why?" I asked.
He then turned to my mother and asked, "May I speak to Syanne alone for a couple of minutes? I just have a few questions that I need to address with her privately, if that's okay."
My mom looked concerned but agreed to leave the room.
"Syanne, I just have a couple of questions to ask you," he said.
"...Okay."
"I noticed that you are very underweight. Do you have any problems with eating?"
"No. I've been sick for the last three days, like I told you earlier; I haven't been able to eat as well. I've always been thin." I replied defensively.

"Okay," he paused. "The reason I ask is because your urine sample came back. It showed that you have ketones in your urine."

"Okay...what is that?" "It is commonly seen in diabetic patients, but you are not diabetic. It is also seen in people who suffer from eating disorders."

I froze. "I hadn't been eating well because I've been sick, so maybe that's why you see these ketones."

"You are also very underweight, Miss Centeno. It is normal for someone your height and age to be between 110 lbs. and 125 lbs. it is not normal for someone your age to be 91 lbs." He sternly replied.

"I'm just naturally skinny. My dad was the same way when he was my age." I just wasn't going to give up without a fight.

He ignored my statement and said, "Have you ever skipped meals to try to lose weight?"

I was silent, but shook my head "no." I'm sure that by this point, I was easy to read.

"Okay. I'm going to call your mom back into the room to explain the findings of the tests." He said.

I nodded. I was sure that I would be forced to eat now.

My mom came in, and he explained to her that ketones are often seen in diabetic patients or in someone who has been starving.

"Does your daughter ever skip meals?" He asked.

"Yes, she has." She answered.

"We have reason to believe that she could be suffering from Anorexia Nervosa." He explained, "In addition to her urine findings, she is also very underweight."

My mom appeared to be embarrassed, and concerned.

He continued, "It is best for her that you consult with a psychologist and a nutritionist. Eating disorders are very serious mental illnesses."

My mom said that she is working with me at home to help correct my behavior because she couldn't afford to have me see a professional at the moment.

"From now on I will watch her and make sure she eats." She promised the doctor.

Her cheeks were turning red. I speculated that it was likely from shame, devastation and even frustration with my behavior. She knew that I had a problem, but I don't think she ever imagined that it was becoming a huge predicament.

"Once she finishes this IV bag, we will release her to you under the notion that you will provide her with the support that she needs. While we do think that this is also the flu, it was worsened by her eating disorder. Please return if any symptoms worsen." He responded with a serious tone.

"At least he still believes it's just flu, and not diet pills and laxatives", I thought to myself.

After I finished my IV bag, we signed some paperwork and I was allowed to leave. My mom was to watch me as I eat from then on.

Watched

Ever since my trip to the E.R, my parents began watching me to make sure that I ate.

I stopped taking diet pills and only took the laxatives when I felt overwhelmed with the calories. These two methods did help me lose and maintain a low weight, but it was too risky. Since that incident, I had no choice I had to eat. If I didn't, I wouldn't be allowed to see my friends. They also said that if I refused, they would take me back to the ER.

My mom also found my scale and hid it from me. I was devastated and angry.

I had some tricks up my sleeve to make it appear like I ate well enough to be able to see my friends. I asked them not to mix my food together, even if it's something like spaghetti and meat sauce or rice and beans. They didn't think anything of it and always did it for me. They were just happy that I was eating.

I always wanted my food to be separated.

First of all, I didn't like the idea of food being mixed together. Secondly, it made it easier to push my food around my plate. Pushing your food around your plate to make it look like you ate is one of the oldest tricks in the eating disorder book. Virtually every teenage girl knew this trick.

I had a very important ritual that I followed when eating any meals. I'd take my knife, and cut up my food into teeny, tiny pieces. I'd then take a big gulp of my water. I would sigh, and stare at my food for a moment. I would then take another big gulp of water. Sigh again. Would take my fork and begin pushing my food around.

I'd stab my food with my fork, and put a little bit of it into my mouth. I would count each time I'd chew, trying to get to 100 before it completely liquefied. If I were constantly chewing my parents would think that I was eating when they'd glance up at me during meals. I would swallow the liquefied food. I would pick up my glass of water a third time and take another drink of water. I'd repeat all of these steps again. Eventually, I started to spit my food out into a napkin. I'd wipe my mouth with the napkin and would discreetly spit out the food. I'd fold the napkin so that you couldn't see the half-chewed up food that I just got rid of. I was successful with this every time. I then found another way to get rid of more food while I ate. I'd say, "I'm going to go pee real quick," or "I'm going to go get another napkin" and would spit the food out in the trashcan or toilet as I went to "use the bathroom." I usually did actually grab another napkin so that I could spit in it throughout my meal, so that wasn't a total lie. Though I did my best to rid myself of unnecessary calories, it just wasn't enough to maintain my low weight.

Changes

Almost a year had passed, and I ended up gaining all of the weight back -- plus more. My parents stopped watching me as closely because I had won over their trust again.
I knew that I had gained the weight back because, first of all, it was blatantly evident. I just didn't know how much trust I'd actually gained back. My friends were supportive of my weight gain and it made me feel good. I even had a boyfriend.
My life had improved within those last few months but I never felt quite right. I was missing something. I was missing Ana.
 I became curious about my weight so I snooped around the house looking for my scale while my mother was at work one afternoon. I found it stashed away in her closet behind some boxes. Though you couldn't immediately see it, if you moved the boxes around you would catch a glimpse of it. I had gained 11 lbs. back. My stomach dropped to the floor. I started to secretly weigh myself after school a few times a week.
 And then my habits slowly began returning. I started eating only half of my sandwiches during lunch, and would throw the rest away. I started to restrict my soda intake and pushing my food around again during dinnertime. I was struggling but I was still fighting to maintain wellness. I didn't completely return to my eating disorder until I received life-changing news a few months later. The news was devastating.

Bad News

I was now fifteen years old, and had formed close bonds with like-minded friends. They weren't just my friends, they were also my family. I spent every waking moment with them and I loved each of them like family.

It is difficult to put into words the overwhelming negative feelings I developed upon receiving the news that I would be moving all the way across the country to the state of Maryland. I did not know anything about Maryland and never, ever thought about this state. To be honest, I forgot it even existed in our country. As soon as I found out, I called each of my friends.

"I'm moving to Maryland." I calmly told them. I believe that my unusual calmness was due to shock and I was completely numb. Their immediate response was denial, and disbelief. The longer we all spoke, the more reality set in. The end of each conversation with each one of my friends ended with tears. My friend, Sarah, even tried to devise a plan where I would just live with her and her family so that I wouldn't have to move.

You can probably imagine how that went over with my parents. The idea never stood a chance but I was anxiously trying everything. I felt so helpless, alone and out of control. I had no say, no influence on the decision my parents made to leave California. I sunk into a deeper depression and sought refuge in the arms of Anorexia Nervosa.

At this point, I became completely consumed by Ana and had dropped to 87 pounds by the spring of 2007. The only thoughts I had were about how I could lose weight even faster. My dreams were filled with perfect, bouncing images of skeletons and mirrors. It was a distraction from the pain I felt from moving once again. Anorexia was the answer.

I was no longer me. I became Anorexia.

I now understand that I fell deeper into my eating disorder in an effort to be in control. I could not control what was going on around me but I could control what I put in my body.

As the day of the move drew nearer and nearer, I clung onto Ana for comfort, my darkest days in view just above the horizon.

Becoming Ana

Ana completely took over in the spring of 2007, where I no longer saw the world, I only saw Ana. My diaries were filled with endless amounts of diet tips and my eating transgressions. Each day, I would log what I consumed and how many calories my meals were. Most days I consumed about 500 calories. As my disorder progressed, this number would decrease rapidly within the coming months. In addition to aggressively monitoring my caloric intake, I was also running a few miles a week.

I only ate to give myself enough strength to keep myself from fainting in between runs. Each time I would run, I would also stop at the coffee shop in town for coffee. I only drank it black during this time to avoid consuming calories and fat. My purpose behind drinking it was to keep my energy up enough to run the mile and a half back home.

Anything that went in my body was only to keep myself alive long enough to continue to starve myself. In other words, I only ate so that I could starve more. Starving was my purpose. It was a dangerous and unhealthy cycle. My only concern was reaching my goal weight. Nothing else mattered. Instead of trusting the Lord with the news of the move, I chose to trust Ana instead.

Rituals

Receiving the news of moving destroyed me. I counted down the days that I would have to say goodbye to everyone that I loved. My life became not just about counting down the days or counting calories. I also counted the number of times I chewed my food. I always tried to get to 100 for each bite of food from my fork. I believed that doing this would trick my brain into thinking that I ate more than I actually did. Within this time, I also learned to chew my food and spit it out in my napkin whenever I had to eat at the table with my family.
I had a specific ritual that would go along with this. Before I'd get to the table, I would grab two or three napkins, then sit down. I was sure to watch everyone to make sure that they weren't watching me. I would then take as small of a bite as possible. Then I would begin to count.

One...two...three...until I got to 100. I'd then discreetly grab one of my napkins, spit out what I had chewed, and roll up the napkin in my hand. I'd drink one big gulp of water and excuse myself to get more water. As I walked into the kitchen, I'd glance behind me to make sure that no one was watching, quickly drop the rolled up napkin in the trash bin, refill my water cup, and would return the table. I would continue to do this over and over again until my plate began to look empty. If there was a lot left, I would cut up the food into tiny pieces, and spread it around on my plate. My parents knew that I struggled to eat so they looked at my plate and praised me for eating well. Little did they know that it was just an illusion, one of the many deceptive tricks taught to me by Ana. I got away with it as long as I could until my body began to show signs of malnutrition.

You're Sick

"You're sick" were the words said to me by the ER doctor in the middle of the winter of 2007. I had lost a significant amount of weight since the news of the move and spent most of my days in a haze from the starvation. Us anorexics would call this "Ana's high".

My first visit to the emergency room was caused by Anorexia Nervosa. I had become very weak and had fainted one sunny day after school. I had never really fainted before but had come close many times before this day.

I had not only been depriving myself of food but I had begun limiting my water intake as well. I did this because I had started to make up these delusions in my mind that water did, in fact, have calories in it despite what all of the scientists said. They were all liars in my mind. It was all a conspiracy to make us all fat.

Clearly, that makes absolutely no rational or logical sense at all. But I was not well. I had spent such a significant amount of time on pro-anorexia websites that I had become brainwashed by all of the lies that had been fed to me by other users online. These websites were more to me than a place to vent, a place to obtain diet tips or a place to learn how to hide my dangerous habits. Pro-anorexia websites became my Bible, my way of living. If I were to die from Anorexia, that was okay by me. Because at least I died trying- and that satisfied my disorder.

I could no longer hear God's voice, as I had spent so long pushing it away and ignoring His word. God to me literally became Anorexia, the only voice I heard, the voice that would eventually lead me to my deathbed.

My first visit to the hospital was a short one, for just a few hours. I was extremely dehydrated and my electrolytes were completely out of balance.

After I finished two large IV bags, the doctor came in and asked my mother to step out of the room to ask me a series of questions. After giving a look of uncertainty, she agreed and stepped outside.

The doctor, whose name I can't recall, was a very kind, tall man in his 50's with dirty blonde hair. There was a nurse with him who held a clipboard, which I assume were the questions that needed to be asked. She had a very serious look on her face, and couldn't have been older than 25.
He began. "Syanne, I hope you're feeling better. I have some questions I'd like to ask you. Is that okay?"
I nodded yes.
"Thank you. Just answer them as honestly as you can and the best that you can, okay?"
Again I nodded yes, not having any idea what types of questions were headed my way.
The first question was asked. "Do you feel safe at home?"
I looked at him confused but answered, "of course, yes!"
"Good," he responded. He continued. "Do you ever have thoughts of hurting yourself or other people?"
I paused.
"I'm always a danger to myself", I thought.
"No, I have never had thoughts of hurting others." I confidently answered.
I was slightly taken aback by this question. I started to sense what was going on.
"Do you have thoughts of hurting yourself, Syanne?" the doctor asked.
Again I paused. But this time, it was longer than just a few seconds.
I finally answered, "I mean, yes I've thought about it. But I haven't done anything."
I kept my relationship with self-mutilation private, as I felt it kept me sane, while I struggled with pleasing Ana.
"What thoughts do you have?" he inquired.
"Great, I should've kept my mouth shut," I thought.
"You know, normal thoughts that teenagers have, I guess." I nervously replied.
"Can you be more specific?"
Again I paused. Should I lie? Was he already onto me? What do I do?

"I'm sorry, I'm just thinking," I said. I was in a mental panic.
"It's okay, you can take your time."
He was so caring. I decided I would offer him part of the truth. He didn't have to know it all, and maybe if I gave him a glimpse of the truth he would stop. Then I wouldn't have to tell him all of it.
"Sometimes I don't really like eating," I told him.
 I thought telling him about my issues with food in such a nonchalant way would make him stop questioning me, once he heard that it really is not that big of a deal. I also felt that my issues with self-harm were seen as more severe than simply not eating so I kept that to myself. And I also think that deep down, I wanted him to save me. To take this away so that I could live a normal life. No, not just to live a normal life. So that I could simply JUST LIVE.
I took a deep breath and awaited his response.
"You are very underweight, did you know that?" he gently asked.
"No." I sharply replied.
Whenever someone said this to me, I felt that it was a lie. Ana quickly returned in my thoughts upon hearing this. She was trying to stop me.
"You've already opened your mouth-- now shut up, stupid girl!" Ana said.
"Well, you are significantly underweight, about 28 pounds underweight for your height and age group," He said.
"Well, I'm just small. Some people are just small. I just don't like to eat sometimes, that's all. But I do eat every day." That was a lie. I wasn't very good at lying to doctors, if you couldn't tell by now.
"Have you heard of Anorexia Nervosa, Syanne?"
 "Yes, I have." I answered.
"It's a very serious illness. It can damage your organs like your kidneys and your heart. It can leave you with lasting effects and even kill you."
"Yes, I know." I rudely replied.

"Do you understand that you have to eat to stay well?" He asked.
"Absolutely! I know it can be dangerous, which is why I don't starve myself." I lied, contradicting myself.
"Do you have any issues with your appetite?" He asked.
This was the perfect question to ask me as it helped me to protect my illness, but the wrong question to ask me to save my life. In my experience, I have seen that many health professionals often do not know how to recognize eating disorders or how to treat them.
"I do," I answered. "I guess that's why I don't really like eating. I don't feel hungry very much."
"I understand," the doctor replied sympathetically.
"My daughter struggles with her appetite as well. Let's call your mom back in so that we can discuss our next step to get you eating well again."
I smiled and said, "Okay."
My mother returned to my room and he began talking to us about my lab findings for the tests that were done. I had a urinalysis and blood work done. He explained that my dehydration was likely due to my bad diet and very low weight. My mother nodded in agreement and said that I have had some issues with eating.
"I think she would benefit from seeing a nutritionist to help her develop meal plans appropriate for her appetite issues. In addition, you should consider having her eat six small meals a day instead of three large meals a day," he explained.

My mother agreed that it would be best for me to try to eat six small meals a day. She knew that my issues were deeper than just a problem with my appetite but she chose to keep that within our family. I feel that the issue stemmed deeper than just not being able to afford specialists; I think that my family also felt that it was something that could be controlled amongst us. Again, from my observation and reflection, I think eating disorders were not understood in the early 2000s, and even to this day, they are still not fully understood. In addition, I had kept so much of my behavior a secret from my parents that they did not realize that I could not overcome this alone. After this conversation we left the hospital and I returned home, completely relieved to be able to starve another day.

The Move

The summer of 2007 quickly came and before I knew it, it was time to say goodbye.
I had done this before when I had left the U.S Virgin Islands to move to Southern California, but this time was even more painful than the last. I was no longer a little girl. I was a 15-year-old young woman and my friendships and relationships meant much more to me than just meeting up and playing on the playground during lunch.
They were my support group, my shoulder to cry on, my best friends and most importantly, they were my family. I remember my last day as if it had just happened yesterday.
I woke up sick to my stomach, with my eyelids stuck together. They became stuck because I had cried myself to sleep and would sporadically wake up throughout the night and would cry some more. I had produced so many tears that it literally became like glue that sealed my eyes together. I did not even want to pry them open because then it would mean that I would see that everything that was going on wasn't some nightmare, it was real. And it was actually happening.
As usual, I skipped dinner the night before only this time I wanted to make it known that I wasn't eating. I was no longer keeping it a secret. As wrong as it is, I wanted my parents to know how badly I was hurting. I wanted them to feel what I was feeling. I wanted them to hurt like I was hurting. I was furious with them and the only thing that I felt that I could control was food so I clung on to Ana more than ever before.
My friends had put together a small celebration for me to show me how much they care for me. One of my closest friends even got a gym t-shirt with our school's name on it and had all my classmates from P.E. to sign it. The entire process was very emotional, and every hug from each friend broke my heart. I did not know when I would be seeing them again. I went through the day and night in a huge fog, making my rounds of goodbyes-- each one harder than the last.
When the night had finally come, my celebration was over.

It was time for me to go home for one last night. A group of about five of my closest friends took me home. Once we reached the flight of stairs that would take me to my soon-to-be old condo, we all began to cry. My parents were calling for me to come inside. Our flight was at 5 in the morning, and it was already 11 at night. I ignored their requests for me to come inside. There was nothing they could say that would make me feel worse than I already did. I felt that if it were my last night in California, I would choose when I decided to say goodbye to my friends; it made me feel somewhat in control of the situation.

Once my parents' requests did become hard to ignore, I told my friends it was time for me to go. I looked them all in the eyes, told them each I loved them and hugged them one last time. I climbed the stairs to the very top, where my condo was. I turned around and looked down and saw my friends huddled together in a circle crying and comforting one another. It was at that moment that I felt truly loved for the first time in my life. I yelled out, "I love you" as I looked down, then opened my door and went inside. As you can imagine, I did not sleep that night.

I got up the next morning more determined than ever to lose as much weight as possible. I wanted to be numb from the world and Ana could help me reach that goal.

I skipped breakfast, and only had black coffee bought for me at the airport. I was giving my parents the silent treatment. Most of my responses consisted of head nods.

Once it was time for us to board the plane, I glanced behind me and whispered goodbye to LAX airport. The little things became so important to me while I went through this life-changing event. I took in every last moment I had in California, indulging in every sight and smell around me.

I boarded the plane and closed my eyes. I was exhausted and terribly hungry but found so much peace and comfort within the arms of Anorexia Nervosa. Throughout the flight, I continued denying food. It not only gave me a sense of comfort but also made me feel powerful. I was in control of my body and I was in control of what I put in my mouth, and there was not anything that anyone could say or do that would stop me.

Maryland

Once we made landfall in Maryland, I was completely taken aback by the humidity. It was summer of 2007 and I had never felt that hot and sticky in my entire life. Since I had been seriously fasting, the humidity and heat drained me so much that I struggled to walk. It was at this time that I started to use counting to both keep myself conscious and to cope with times of mental chaos.

We drove through our new town and I was incredibly dissatisfied with the appearance of my surroundings. There was so much that I disliked about Maryland. I particularly disliked the fact that nothing was within walking distance and that my new house was 30 minutes away from civilization. Back home in California everything was within walking and running distance. I also disliked the aesthetics of the buildings; I felt that everything was just so "country" when I had become accustomed to suburban life. I was completely shocked when I saw real-life Amish people. I had never seen one in my life.

But there were a few benefits. One thing that I did immediately like was the house that my parents had bought. I had never lived in such a big house before and I had never had my own room before. I found solace in my room and decorated it with images of Audrey Hepburn and Marilyn Monroe, two women that I admired for their strength in battling adversity and tough times.

In time, I also filled my walls with images of emaciated models that I had pulled from high fashion magazines. The corner of my room where the images were hung became a shrine for Ana, a place that I could worship my sick habits. I spent much of my time in my Ana shrine, meditating in an effort to discipline my mind enough to continue to starve.

Starving during my first summer in Maryland was easy. I did not have any friends to spend my time with and school was out so I was able to focus all of my energy into my unhealthy obsessions with food. I spent most of my days reading memoirs about Anorexia Nervosa. These books made me feel like I was not alone in my suffering.

Talking to my friends was difficult because of the 3-hour time difference between the east coast and west coast. They called me as much as they could but it wasn't long before I started to feel like they were forgetting about me. I slipped into the deepest, darkest depression of my life and felt utterly alone.

You're probably wondering, what about your parents? I never felt that I could talk to my parents about how I was feeling because they often became frustrated with hearing me repeat that I was unhappy over and over. They always tried their best to help me and I was ungrateful. Eventually, I completely lost the desire to confide in them about anything. My sister and I weren't really close, and she kept to herself most days. She was struggling with the emotions of the move as well.

I always wondered how in the world it was possible to feel so alone in a house full of people but it's easy when those around you lack understanding in the battles you are going through. I felt that my parents had each other to get through a hard time but I had no one. Sure, they were there physically but it was difficult for me to connect with them on a deep emotional level. I had a very hard time trusting them with my feelings.

As time went by, the wedge between my parents and I grew. I was often on edge. It wasn't just because of the move; it was also because my body wasn't getting the nutrients it needed. I became so depressed that my parents ended up sending me back to California for part of the summer until school began. They did this in an effort to relieve some of my depression. Seeing my friends did alleviate a lot of my sadness but I still clung onto Anorexia. Instead of being grateful to see my friends again, I tried to develop yet another plan to live in California with my friends.
Once again, that did not work in my favor. I returned to Maryland a little bit more depressed than I was before. At this point, I was only two weeks away from starting tenth grade in my new school. I was terrified that I would experience the same thing that I had experienced when I was the new girl in third grade. But that didn't happen this time.

New Girl

Starting a new school all over again was one of my worst fears...and here I was doing it again. When I walked into my new school, I was overwhelmed. It was much bigger than my high school back in Oak Park and also much more diverse. There were hundreds of more students at this school than there was in my old school. Most people seemed to keep to themselves but it was easy to distinguish who the popular kids were and who was not. I was not sure where I stood yet in the social hierarchy, but I presumed that I would be one of the unpopular kids like I was when I had moved to California. During lunch on my first day, I saw a shy, kind-looking boy who was standing next to a table by himself. I didn't want to be alone at lunch like I was the last time I moved so I mustered up the courage to approach him.
I introduced myself and he told me his name was Eric.
"Are you new too?" I asked him, curiously.
"No, I'm actually just waiting for my friends. I'll introduce you to them!" He excitedly replied.

While we waited for his friends, I told him about California and about how I was forced to move to Maryland against my will.
"Do you like it here so far, though?" he asked.
I smiled and said, "No. Not really."
Before I could explain why, his friends arrived. I noticed that they were different than the rest of the kids at my school. They wore anime-inspired clothing with cattails and big bows. I was taken aback but immediately liked them because I was also an anime fan. They were so welcoming and friendly. I sat down with them while they ate lunch and talked about anime, Maryland and life in California. One of the girls in the group noticed that I wasn't eating and asked me if I was hungry.
 "I don't really eat," I told her.
 "Why not?" She asked as she wrinkled her nose.
"Because, I don't have the desire to." I stated.
"Hmm. Well, that's interesting." was her only reply.
She didn't seem to be concerned about it.
She was very thin, so I was hoping that maybe she was a fellow Ana worshipper as well. It appeared that she didn't know anything about self-starvation or eating disorders.
From then on I decided to keep it to myself unless someone brought it up to me first.
I spent a lot of time with their group and became very close to many of them, however, these friendships were short-lived.
I wanted nothing more than to be popular and hang out with the cool kids. I did not want to go through the bullying I had faced in elementary school and was willing to do anything to avoid it. I was even willing tp desert those who welcomed me when I didn't have anyone else. I was selfish and I was only interested in self-gratification and my social status.
It wasn't long until I started to become friends with the most popular girl in my grade during my 10th grade English class. She was a beautiful, blonde, cheerleader named Tracy with a country accent. Instead of saying, "wash" she would say "warsh" because of her accent. I thought it was funny, yet I wanted to be like her. All the boys liked her and all the girls seemed to want to be her friend.

That's why I was in complete astonishment when she approached me. I was even more astonished that she invited me to have lunch with her every day. During those lunches, I ended up meeting the other "cool" kids, which consisted of football players, cheerleaders and skaters. Most days I could not believe that I was sitting amongst the type of people that I had wanted to be like my entire life.

I ended up ditching my "strange" friends for good for an opportunity to become a mainstream popular girl. Even now, I can't forgive myself for ignoring them like I never knew them. Now as an adult, I would never do that. But at the time, I couldn't see the world beyond high school and Anorexia. Teenagers are selfish, and I certainly was no different.

One day, Tracy was eating the school lunch, which contained curly fries and chicken nuggets. As she ate them, she began to complain.

She said, "I really need to stop eating this crap- I'm like one of the fatter girls on our cheerleading squad."

I rolled my eyes at her and said, "You're not fat, obviously. Stop."

She looked down to see what I was eating and then realized that I was not eating anything.

"Hey", she began. "Do you ever eat lunch? Like, do you ever eat anything? You've been here for five months and I swear I never see you eat. That's why you're super skinny."

"Exactly," I winked.

"Wait, what do you mean?" She asked with a grin.

"I don't know if I should tell you. Can I trust you?" I asked her with suspicion in my voice.

"Yes! I won't tell!" she answered anxiously.

"Okay", I proceeded.

"Have you ever heard of Anorexia, or any eating disorder?" I asked.

She replied, "Yeah, I use to make myself throw up. But I stopped for a while. Why, do you do that too?"

I then said, "well, not throw up but I did do that a few times when I gave in to hunger. I prefer to starve. It feels great, and I look great too!"
"How do you do that? I literally can't get myself to just not eat!" she replied eagerly.
"Honestly, I don't really know. I've fainted after not eating before. It's really hard, but I just don't eat."
 I paused for a moment and continued.
 "If I feel like eating, I just go do something else, or chew gum. I'll also drink black coffee if it gets really bad."
 "But you obviously eat because you're not like grossly thin," she bluntly said.
This comment enraged me, though I knew she didn't mean to offend me. I mean, who would want to look grossly thin, right? But looking "grossly thin" was my goal. If I looked emaciated and frail, that would mean that I was satisfying Ana and that I was doing an extraordinary job at controlling what I allowed into my body. It's not that I thought I was fat but I strived to be as shockingly thin as possible. Getting there would be a true test of willpower and after hearing her say that, I knew I had to prove myself. Her comment ringed in my ears throughout the day, and I was even more driven to lose as much weight as I could, even if it resulted in death.

Fitting In

After getting to know Tracy and the other popular kids more, I found them to be quite boring. All they wanted to do was go to parties. I had no interest in parties for two reasons. One, I didn't like meeting new people and felt awkward doing it and two, parties were usually full of food and I needed to avoid any temptation to eat. Not to mention that these parties were full of alcohol and everyone knows that alcohol is full of calories.

I began hanging out with the "alternative" kids, who were neither popular nor unpopular. They kind of floated through the crowds, unbothered and unaffected. Most of this group consisted of musicians, artists and writers. They were deep thinkers and weren't into partying, either. I immediately fit into this group, as I was also a musician and an artist.

I poured my heart out into sketchbooks with drawings that had hidden meanings. Most of my sketches were about Ana, while others were about depression and impulse. My friends would often share their drawings, paintings and poems with one another. I also did share my art occasionally, but feared being critiqued by the others. Their talent was unbelievable. When I would draw, I didn't focus on aesthetic appeal as much as I focused on the message that I was trying to convey. It wasn't realism-- it was a mixture of fantasy, abstract, and macabre artistic themes.

Music was also my safe haven. I played guitar and clarinet, and would later begin playing the piano. I ended up joining a band with one of the alternative kids. I think it was called Genesis 303. The name was supposed to signify a computer crash or something, I don't really know. I was the only girl and had the most incredible time creating music with such a gifted group of kids. When I played my guitar and sang, I forgot about everything. Even Ana.

I would stay after school as long as possible to escape as long as I possibly could from Ana. Yes, I loved Ana, but by this point, I no longer felt in control. My parents had decided that my unwillingness to eat was reaching dangerous levels, so they hired a therapist in desperation, hoping she could save me. Dr. Mouler was tall like a skyscraper, pushing six feet and thin like a prima ballerina. She had short, silver hair, a bright smile, and wore dark, grey-framed glasses. I instantly liked her. I found her to be warm and inviting. What I loved most about having a therapist was that I could say virtually anything and not one thing I said would leave the room. She was sworn to confidentiality and secrecy and I found solace in that. I could finally say what I meant without the fear that somehow it would get out, or that I would be judged on it. For once, I felt safe in talking about how I really viewed myself and the world around me. She quickly became one of my favorite people. While I was seeing Dr. Mouler, I began to improve during the first few months of therapy. I started eating once or twice a day and stopped weighing myself. The doctor had directed my parents to hide the scale so that I wouldn't be tempted to compulsively check my weight every day. Everyone started noticing my weight gain and commented on how "healthy" I looked. It felt good for a while to receive a positive comment, but after a couple of months, I began to panic.

"Healthy? Healthy isn't good. Healthy means fat, and out of control." Ana told me. I fought against Ana as hard as I could, but then very rapidly began losing my way.

 I relapsed out of the blue one day, with no real trigger. I just felt that I could not continue eating. I had enough of trying. And that's the thing about Anorexia. You think she's gone, but then she sneaks up on you without notice. Just like that, in a blink of an eye, Ana was back with a vengeance.

She's Back

I soon realized that Ana never left. She had simply been hibernating, re-energizing, and waiting for her opportunity to return stronger than ever before. Once again, I returned to days of fasting, going as many days as I could without eating a morsel of food. If I felt ill, I'd have a glass of soymilk to keep me conscious. I usually ended up eating a few crackers by the 5th day. Then I'd immediately return to another week long fast. When I visited my therapist after my first week of fasting, I told her absolutely everything. I couldn't explain to her why I relapsed; I didn't have an explanation. I just knew that I had woken up a few days before and suddenly didn't feel like trying anymore. Eating always took a lot of mental preparation and I soon became exhausted from the process of eating. Maybe I just lost the strength to try. Ana woke up, and she didn't want to let me go this time.

Dr. Mouler encouraged me to eat, and gave me a million reasons why I should. She also told me a million more reasons as to why I should live. After an hour-long lecture from my therapist, I felt empowered to get better.

"I haven't eaten in five days. But I'm not too far gone to getting better." I thought to myself.

So one day after one of my inspiring therapy sessions, I asked my mom to take me to the pizza restaurant down the street.

"Are you actually going to eat it?" she asked.

"Oh yes, I'm ready to be healthy. I'm ready to eat this time." I confidently answered.

She agreed to take me and we stopped at the nearest pizza restaurant and picked up a large Italian sausage pizza. Since I hadn't eaten in days, I was anxious to start eating-- and I wasted no time in doing so. Within a few minutes, I had devoured half of the large pizza by myself.

"Sy, take it easy!" my mom exclaimed with worry in her voice. I was ravenous. I couldn't stop.

Before I knew it, I had consumed the entire large pizza by myself, except for one piece. My stomach was bloated, and I felt like I couldn't breathe due to my most recent binge. Then Ana crept back into my mind.

"Throw it up...you know you were not supposed to do that. You must be empty. Now you'll have to fast for more than five days. Get rid of it--now!" Once I got home, I ran to my room, and lay on my bed with my eyes close tightly, trying my best to resist Ana's voice.

"Get rid of it now, get rid of it now!" I heard Ana yell over and over again.

I began to sob and lost what was left of my control over my life. I felt guilt and disgust for ruining my week long fast at Ana's request. The amount of guilt I felt was unbearable. I became suicidal within minutes, all because I ate an entire pizza. I was literally starving but I could not get myself to be content with having any food in my body.

I felt that I had no choice but to purge the pizza that I had eaten. With mascara running down my face, I stumbled my way into the bathroom and instantly felt nauseous. I wasn't nauseous because I was physically ill from the pizza; I was nauseous because I was so disgusted with myself that I literally became sick. When I purged the pizza, I barely had to try-- it just sort of fell out. I hated the way it felt, but it was better to me than having to feel food in my stomach. After I finished, I rinsed my mouth out, sprayed myself with perfume to mask the odor of vomit and then quietly walked back to my bed.

As I lay in bed, I reflected on what I had done. I had performed my first real binge and purge in a state of desperation. I was not a fan of this routine but if I felt that I had absolutely no choice, I would binge and purge. I would usually do this after days and days of long fasts. Once I'd see my therapist, I'd feel "inspired" to get better...but within minutes of binging (when I'd swore I'd get better), I would purge. By the third time that I repeated this act, I decided that I would tell my therapist about it. It had become too routine and too normal. I was terrified and no longer wanted to continue purging. It wasn't the same as starving; Bulimia was not my eating disorder of choice. I didn't feel nearly as comfortable with it as I've felt with Ana.

"I've been binging and purging" were the first words that came out of my mouth as I stepped into Dr. Mouler's office.

"Why do you feel that you need to do that?" She asked.

"Well, I leave out of here feeling so great and ready for recovery...so I get my mom to stop at a pizza place." I paused for a moment. "I became motivated to get better, and get a large pizza all for myself. But then after I eat it, I feel guilty and like, ashamed."

"So you purge?" Dr. Mouler inquired.

"Yeah," I shamefully replied.

"Have you ever experimented with bulimia before?" she asked.

"Yes, a couple of times. But those were conscious decisions. When I eat the pizza, I literally feel like I can't stop, and when I'm done, I can feel my stomach protruding. The look of it makes me sick and I mean literally sick to where I became nauseous with disgust for myself and I go to the bathroom and very easily throw up." I explained.

"Okay, I understand. You need to stop binging and purging. Engaging in this behavior, especially after days of fasting can be terribly dangerous. Why don't you initiate your road to recovery by starting off with six small meals a day?" she said to me with encouragement in her voice.

"I just don't know if I can do that. I feel stuck. I'm tired of fighting with these eating disorders, but I feel like I'm addicted. I can't think of anything else," I confided in her with despair in my voice.

"That's what eating disorders do," she said. "They are like parasites. They make themselves at home in your mind and eventually become hosts and obtain control over your entire being. They can be very difficult to overcome because of their complexities. But I have faith in you, Syanne, that you WILL overcome this."

Even though she believed in me, I just knew that things would only worsen. I liked Ana because she made me feel in control, but this was to the point to where I couldn't even think for myself. Anorexia Nervosa may just be a mental illness to most; just a manifestation made up by the mind. But to me, Anorexia Nervosa was a living being that made herself at home in my mind, and in my soul. Every battle I had within myself never felt as if I was just arguing with myself. Instead, it felt as if I was debating with a real, breathing person. Ana was like the devil on my left shoulder, while the part of my brain that was still well was the angel on my right shoulder. The angel always lost and Ana became stronger and stronger until there was no more room for the angel. This was the way that I would often explain my eating disorder to healthcare professionals.

Ana was quite literally consuming my brain, my bones, my organs and my soul. There was no room for much else. I left my therapist's office that day determined to end my binging and purging habit. And I have to say; I succeeded in stopping that behavior. But the only way I was able to do that was to continue my relationship with Ana. If I had nothing in my stomach, then I would have nothing to purge. So I went on my first ever two-week fast.

Fasting

When I went on my first two-week fast, I did not anticipate how long it would be. Two weeks was just what I had gotten to. My goal was to fast for as long as I possibly could. I had set rules in how I would do this so that I could lose as much weight as possible but survive to see my success. I started my fast directly after seeing my therapist the previous Friday. I could drink soymilk once a day and eat crackers with soymilk on every fourth day. I was "allowed" to eat sautéed cauliflower every Friday. Doing this kept me significantly under 1,000 calories per week.
The first week was relatively easy. I did not eat anything for the first week; all I did was drink black coffee throughout the day to keep myself from feeling too hungry. "Lucky" for me, black coffee has no calories. Every day, I woke up with a headache similar to that of a hangover. My head was spinning and throbbing. I speculate it was from both starvation and too much caffeine.
My parents knew what I was doing and they were in a state of panic. Every day they tried to encourage me to eat and would sometimes try to bribe me with rewards. I never gave in. No reward was greater than the satisfaction of Ana.
At the end of each day, I would drink a glass of soymilk. Before I would go to bed I would lie on my bedroom floor and proceed to complete 300 sit-ups. I'd count in 3 sets of 100. By the end of the second set, my chest would begin aching and it would get hard to breathe. Despite this, I would push through my third set and by the time I was counting in the 90's, I was blacking out. As soon as I was done, I'd lay on the floor for up to ten minutes until I gathered the strength to get myself up into my bed. I was so weak.
After my first week of fasting and eating nothing at all, I went into my therapist's office the following Friday. My mother had asked to come in with me because she wanted to discuss my plummeting mental state.

"She hasn't eaten anything in over a week", my mom told her as her voice broke.

I stayed silent. I was no longer present in my own body.

"Syanne, why are you not eating?"" Dr. Mouler asked.

I sighed and said, "I just can't. No matter what, I can't."

"Yes you can. You are in control, don't let the disorder win," She told me.

"I think she has lost all of her control over this," My mother quietly said.

"Well, if we see no improvement over the next week or so, then I recommend in-patient hospitalization." She responded.

My stomach dropped, and my eyes widened.

"Hospitalization? No, you can't let this happen!" Ana screamed.

"But is a hospitalization really necessary? I'm not that sick!" I said in a panic.

"Syanne." Dr. Mouler began to say, "You are emaciated. You are dangerously thin. And do you know how I know you aren't well? Because you can't see that you are seriously ill."

My mom nodded in agreement. I stayed silent while they both just stared at me, looking at me as if it was the last time they'd see me alive. I felt immediate shame and embarrassment for the first time ever.

My mom ended up leaving the room, and Dr. Mouler and I began talking about different methods I could try on my own to overcome Ana. I was numb the entire time. I knew that I wasn't going to follow any of her suggestions. Ana had me as her sacrifice and I was going to die. I weighed 85 pounds.

After I left my therapy session, I rode in the car with my mother back home. For the first 15 minutes, it was piercingly quiet. I could see in my mom's face that she was contemplating the decision to send me to an inpatient eating disorder clinic. I told her I was sorry that it had come to this but I just could not stop.

"If you don't start eating by your next therapy session, I'm going to have no choice but to hospitalize you." She calmly told me. Her voice was soothing, but I could tell that she was heartbroken inside. Her face was red, and her lips were trembling.
"I know. I will fight with everything inside of me to get better on my own. But I don't think that there's much of me left." I shamefully told her.
"I know, I know." My mother replied.
All hope was gone. She and I both knew that Ana had a dangerous hold on me, and she was not going to go down without a fight. My next week of fasting proved to be my most dangerous fast yet.

Fasting Pt. 2

My second week of fasting was unbearable. I had a few crackers throughout the week, but also began exercising compulsively. I would often go to the kitchen and smell food when I was hungry; it was some sort of sick self-torture. Ana liked to tease me with what I couldn't have. I wanted to eat so badly but just could not get myself to do it. Ana wouldn't let me and I had to obey her every request, no matter what.

In present time, I often refer to the Anorexia as a demon who had invaded my space. There is no better way to explain it because she possessed my mind, body and soul. She wasn't me but I became her. I was Ana, walking in the flesh with nothing but bones holding my body together.

By the end of the week, I fell to 81 pounds. I spent all week out of school, laying in bed with no strength left. I was dying. I laid in my mom's bed, and she would bring me plain chicken broth. It's the only thing I would consume as it had no calories but had the electrolytes I needed to stay alert longer. My eyes were almost always closed and when I had to get up, it took everything in me to move each leg. I felt as if I was literally dragging my body behind me. All I wanted to do was lay in bed with Ana's high. Everything around me always appeared to be spinning and I had a constant, fluttering feeling in my chest. It felt like adrenaline, even though I was lying in bed perfectly still. In hindsight, I realize that it was my heart struggling to maintain life.

I had been very aggressive with my body that second week. I tried my best to lose as much weight as possible before Friday. If I was going to go into the hospital, as my therapist had discussed, then I had to quickly meet Ana's requirements before all of my hard work was stolen from me.

As I've said before, Ana was not going to go down without a fight. I was always visually in a fog but my hearing was intensified. The echoes created by severe hunger made the world sound louder. I spent the last part of the week bedridden, gravely ill and reflecting on how I got to this point. I was not proud of this. I was not happy. And I was in pain both emotionally and physically. *"How did I get here?"* I pondered in my silence.
"My God, what happened? Why did I do this? Why didn't you save me?" I could feel my tears streaming down my face. Ana had conquered me, she won the battle and I was losing life.
For the first time in a long time, I talked to God. But in all honesty, I wasn't talking. I was angry, yelling at Him and cursing. *"How could you leave me? Why didn't you help me? Why me? What did I do wrong?"* As I asked these questions in private conversation with God, I heard no response.
I wept and pleaded with God to help me. Again, no response. I soon quickly fell asleep, quietly weeping in my bed, angry with myself and angry with God.
I soon woke up in a daze, my eyes barely open. It took too much strength to keep them open. Because of my intensified hearing caused by the starvation, I could hear my parents talking all the way downstairs as clear as day.
"She's not doing well," my mom told my dad.
He agreed with her.
"It's time to put her in the hospital. We don't have any other options. Let's just do it," my dad said.
I could feel Ana becoming frantic and my heart began to race. She was furious and forced me to sit up in bed with the little bit of strength I had left.

As my heart was beating faster and faster, I suddenly started sweating and felt hot. My breathing became heavier and I became nauseous. Then very rapidly, my peripheral vision began to black out and I realized that I was beginning to lose consciousness. I became frantic and realized that it was become terribly difficult to hear within seconds and everything began to sound further and further away. I yelled out for my mother with the absolute last ounce of strength that I had left.

As my eyes closed, I distantly heard the sounds of frenzied footsteps speedily climbing the stairs. Everything I heard sounded like I was listening to all of the voices and sounds underwater. I then felt my mother's hand on my arm as she lifted a bottle of rubbing alcohol to my nose, which is used to keep those who are fainting awake and alert.

 I could slowly feel my hearing coming back, my breathing slowed down and I was able to begin opening my eyes. My face was covered in sweat as I looked up to my mother and said, "I don't feel well."

"We have to put you in the hospital," she said. "Tomorrow we are seeing your therapist to see where we go to next. If you start getting too sick, I'm going to take you to the ER. You can't continue like this."

 "I know, I'll be fine until tomorrow. I'll drink the rest of my broth." She sat beside me on the bed as I drifted off to sleep.

It's Time

The next day, I woke up even weaker than the day before. I did not think it was possible to become even weaker, yet there I was still hanging on. While I lay in bed, I pondered everything that had happened the night before. You see, when you fast and your body is literally slowly shutting down, your mind begins to reflect, not just on daily occurrences, but also on your entire life. What you did wrong, what you could have done better in. The natural order of the world, the way every move you make causes a domino effect around you. What certain situations mean and how you get to where you are in present time.

I was expecting to die, and so did my mind, my body and soul. When you feel that you're dying, you spend a large amount of your time looking back and wondering where you would be had things been different. I was daydreaming about how I could be back in school with my friends, having a normal teenage life and having the ability to be active without worrying about passing out. I had begun to forget what that was like.

Most of my day was spent sleeping before I had to see my therapist about my hospitalization.

By this point, I wanted to go. I wanted the opportunity to be happy and to receive the care that I needed to make senses of my thoughts and impulses. I wanted to be normal and most of all I wanted to be happy.

My appointment was at 6 pm, so my mother came upstairs to help me get ready since I had become so weak. All of my clothes were too big for me; size 00 was not small enough and sagged terribly. I was able to fit in a girl's size 12 pants (about the size of a 10-year-old) I had bought at the thrift store, and even that sagged in places. I wore a long-sleeved, xx-small shirt that fell over my body the way it would fall off a clothing hanger. Before we left, I looked in the mirror and began to see just how sick I really was. My shoulder blades were so sharp that it appeared as if they could pierce through my skin. My cheeks were deeply sunk in and when I pulled my shirt to my body to fit, you could see every rib.

I was saddened by what my life had come to, but Ana was pleased. She loved my ghostly, pale appearance...my skeletal frame was impossible to hide. She was proud of my toothpick legs, bony fingers and protruding collarbones. She was even proud of my dry, brittle hair that would break and fall when I'd brush it. I stared at myself for as long as my strength would allow me to stand. I then climbed down the stairs, linked arm and arm with my mother. Walking down those stairs was an eerie experience. The feeling in the house was of impending death, sorrow and despair. In some ways, it felt as if I was walking to my own funeral. I climbed in the car, reclined the seat back and proceeded to Dr. Mouler's office.

The entire car ride was silent, both my mother and I were in deep thought. I imagined she was thinking where she had gone wrong and how on earth I could've ended up this way. Though she never said that, I could easily read it on her face. I felt pure shame and embarrassment for getting this far. And yet, I didn't want to stop. Ana had truly become more important to me than my family, my friends and my own life. I guess that this is why it was time for me to go into treatment.

After arriving to Dr. Mouler's office, the reality of treatment began to sink in.

How long would I be gone? Would they really be forcing me to eat? What will they do with me? Is this really necessary?

These were all questions I asked myself as I waited for Dr. Mouler to pull us into her office. A few minutes later, she walked outside of her office, and called my mother and me to come in. We sat down and began to talk.
"So how have you been doing, Syanne?" She asked with concern in her voice.
"Not too good", I answered.
"I can see that. You don't look well, Syanne. You look very emaciated. You look much worse than last week," She told me, her voice calm and sweet.
"She is not doing well. She didn't drink or eat anything all week. All I could get her to have was chicken broth. That's all she would say, "yes" too. My mother said, her voice shaking.
"Well, chicken broth has zero calories," I added.
She turned to my mom and said, "I think in order to save her life we need to hospitalize her."
My mother's only answer was, "It's time."
"How do you feel about that, Syanne?" she asked.
"I don't know how to feel. But I think you are both right. I feel...out of control, and I feel weak," I told her.
I was so ashamed, there's no other way to express what I felt in words other than by using the word shame.
"The next step is to send your records over to the clinic and get you enrolled as an in-patient patient," Dr. Mouler said. "Let's head over to my computer to get this process started."
I can't remember the entire process but I do remember sitting on my mom's lap as my therapist worked on the computer to get me on the list as a patient in the eating disorder clinic. The way this hospital works was by looking at who was the "sickest". They had a long waiting list but I was able to get in within about four days. I was seen as critical enough to be bumped up to the top of the list. I left my therapist's office feeling like there was still some hope left, that maybe I could finally get rid of Ana and move on towards a healthier, happier life.

October 27th, 2008

I don't know where to begin with this part of my story. This was one of the most difficult things that I have gone through in my 26 years of life. I'm sure you were hoping to read about renewal and a happy ending. But the end of this story is not near yet and this point of my life was not a happy one. The hope I had in recovery was quickly shattered once I entered the doors of this facility.

Before reaching this point, my parents and I had spent our previous four days packing my things, notifying my school and mentally preparing for the big changes ahead. I would be living at this clinic two hours away from my parents with other people like me. My parents wouldn't be able to come and see me every day and that scared me. I was to go on this journey alone.

I woke up on the morning of October 27th, 2008, feeling fearful and anxious about the road ahead. What scared me the most was not knowing how they would treat my eating disorder. I had spent a lot of time reading about eating disorder treatments and patient testimonials online the night before but they did not offer very much insight on what treatments they had received. Most online users wrote about how they were forced to gain weight but didn't receive treatment for the causes of their eating disorders. This terrified me. Could they really force you to gain weight? And there's no way they didn't receive treatment. I figured that they were just bitter about their recovery and the weight gain. I brushed it off and reminded myself that this was one of the best eating disorder clinics in the United States. They knew what they were doing; they knew how to help me. How else would they be the best? It was my time to find out.

My parents, my sister and I all climbed into the car with several of my suitcases in the back filled with brand new clothing items. I had to get an entire new wardrobe because this clinic did not allow clothing with pockets or zippers. Do you know how difficult it can be to find clothing without pockets or zippers? It was nearly impossible. It took us nearly three hours to get to Northern Maryland, which is where the clinic was located.

The entire hospital premises were enormous, stretching out for several miles. We arrived at their main offices, which was further away from the clinic campus.

The office was painted a brownish color with leaves and flowers being the theme of their decorations. It had a very distinct smell, like a mixture of hand sanitizer and flowers...with something else. I use to speculate that the flower scent was used to mask the scent of the decaying, walking corpses that would walk through this building. That's what the "something else" smell was, in my opinion.

My family and I sat near a big window, the sun shining through the trees warming us on that cold, fall day. We were all close together and at that moment I came to realize how much I was going to miss them. They may not have understood me...but I didn't even understand myself. If there was anything I was sure of at that moment, it was that they loved me. I felt that I had let them down and I owed it to them to beat Ana and become the best person that I could be.

At least two hours passed, before we were called back into a smaller office. The office was so small that we all couldn't fit and my dad had to stand in the doorway to make room for all of us. I sat down in one of their "leafy" green chairs, my mom and sister seated to my right. There was a middle-aged woman at the desk. She smiled and was very friendly. She asked a series of questions that took at least an hour. Questions that I had been asked in emergency rooms such as, "Do you feel like you are a danger to yourself or others?" and "Do you abuse alcohol or use illegal drugs?" There were so many questions that there is no way I could remember them all.

From there, we were taken to another room where I received a medical evaluation. I was given some sort of blood pressure test where I would first lay down, sit down, sit up, and then finally stand up all while they were reading my blood pressure results.

They did find that my blood pressure was unstable and very low. They weighed me but made me face away from the scale so that I would not know what it was. They then gave me a blood test, which was painful because they had difficulty finding my vein due to dehydration.

From there we were escorted to yet another room. There was a lot of paperwork that my parents had to fill out and then I received my patient handbook, which contained all the rules for the patients of the clinic. It was then finally time for us to go to the main campus of the hospital, which was about a 10-15 minute drive from the offices.

The main campus of the hospital was even bigger than the exterior of the offices that we had just visited. The structural design of this building was absolutely stunning. It was built out of bricks and then the main entrance resembled a castle, the lawn a bright, green color. I stared in awe as we parked at the front of the building. My dad unloaded my suitcases, and we all made our way to the front door. As I walked in, I took a deep breath and thought, "*this is it, and there's no turning back now.*"

We entered into the lobby, where a large, steel door with locks separated us from the rest of the hospital. We sat and waited for a few minutes until an older woman with short, blonde hair came through the steel doors to greet us with two other women. Her name was Betty; I don't recall the names of the other two. I began to shake as the reality of what was happening sunk in.

At that moment, I turned to my mom and whispered, "I don't want to do this anymore. I can get better on my own."

To which she replied, "You can't do it on your own, and we are here. You have to."

I stayed silent as Betty began to guide us and took us through those steel doors, which slammed behind us and automatically locked on their own.

Betty first took us through the dormitories, showing us the rooms of different patients who were admitted. They were all empty and uncomfortably quiet. She told us a little bit about the girls who lived there. These girls would later become my family. Finally, we stopped at my room, which was the largest room in the hospital. It housed two other girls who were my age. The room was plain, with shelves placed in the center for our things. Betty asked me to stay in the room with the other two women while she showed my parents the rest of the building. I hesitated, but before I knew it she had already taken them away and I was left with my suitcases, afraid, with two women I had never met before. They began to go through my suitcases with no warning. As I stood there watching, one of the women asked me to get undressed.

"Why?" I asked.

"Because we have to make sure you're not carrying any restricted items," one of the women said, rolling her eyes.

"But where are my parents?" I timidly asked.

"They'll be back, but we have to search you." The woman answered, annoyed. I froze for a few seconds as they waited for me to undress.

"Well, come on." She impatiently said.

I started to remove my shirt first and then my pants. I stood there shaking, with my arms crossed around my skeletal frame, hoping that this would quickly be over. But it wasn't.
"You have to remove your underwear and bra as well," one of the women said.
"Why?" I angrily asked.
"Because as we told you before, we have to search you for restricted items," the woman said even more annoyed than before.
I became very nervous. I didn't understand why I needed to be searched completely naked. I hesitantly obeyed, and removed my underwear and bra. I stood there, in the middle of the room completely naked and afraid.
The woman said, "Turn around."
 I turned around very quickly, in a full circle.
She exclaimed, "Wait– wait! Spread your buttocks, please". She was making sure that I "didn't have anything that might cause harm to myself or others".
My hands were shaking as the woman bent down on her knees to examine my most private areas that not one person had seen before. I held my breath and tightly closed my eyes. I was holding in tears and my cheeks were burning. I felt so violated. So exposed. I felt like a prisoner, like someone who had committed a terrible crime at just the age of sixteen-years-old.
After they had finished, they permitted me to get dressed as they confiscated some of my items from my suitcases, which included my iPod. They said these were items that were earned and I could not keep it until they felt I had progressed enough to receive it.
We quietly left my new room, and met up with my parents. My parents were in the living area of the hospital where there were telephones, the nurses' station, a television, and several chairs.

All around me were the patients of the hospital who ranged in age from 13-40 years old. They all seemed to mope around in silence, some crying, others' sat in corners with angry expressions, and a few were playing card games on the floor. The general feeling I got from the other patients around me was hopelessness and desperation.

I was very quiet, so my mom turned to me and said, "Are you okay? What'd they do downstairs?"

My eyes began to water and I looked at her and whispered, "They searched me."

She instantly became angry. "Wait, they searched you? How?"

"They made me take my clothes off," I said.

"Leaving you in your bra and underwear?" She exclaimed.

"No, they made me take those off too."

She was in complete shock, and apologized to me. My parents had no idea that they would be searching me at all, nonetheless completely naked! My dad immediately asked to speak with Betty. She proceeded to explain to him that this was in the paperwork we had signed and it was a necessary routine because girls have come in with diet pills, drugs and items stored in their rectums. He said that I was only sixteen-years-old and had answered the series of questions that included questions about diet pills, drugs and other items. Her only response was that it was necessary and that we agreed to the process once we signed the paperwork. There was no use in arguing with them so my parents simply told them not to do it again, at least not without their knowledge.

Night quickly fell upon us, and it was time to say goodbye. Before my parents left, I told them that I needed to use the restroom-- I had not been able to go for hours. They told me to ask one of the orderlies where the restroom was. I approached a man in his 30's, who was balding, with glasses.

"Hi, I need to use the restroom please, where is it?" I kindly asked him.

"No, there are no restroom breaks at this time," He replied.

"But I haven't gone all day, I just got here," I explained.

"We only allow 3-4 restroom breaks during designated times throughout the day." He robotically stated.

I walked away and approached my dad and told him what had happened. At this point, he became enraged and loudly said, "What the hell is wrong with these people?"

He instantly went up to the male orderly and assertively told him that I needed to use the restroom now; I was new and was not there all day to follow their normal routine.

The orderly responded with, "Okay, but she cannot do this tomorrow."

The male orderly stepped into the restroom with me as I entered a stall and did my business. When I was finished, I turned around to flush the toilet but was surprised to see that there was no handle to flush. Instead, there was a keyhole. I quickly understood that we could not flush our own toilets and that the orderlies would have to inspect the toilets after we were finished. While I walked out of the stall to wash my hands, he entered the stall I had been in. I watched him in the mirror, curious to see how this whole thing worked.

It was quite simple, he simply inserted the key, turned it and the toilet immediately flushed. I had never seen anything like that before.

After using the restroom, the orderly took me to the dining area where I was to eat dinner. But first, my family had to leave. I hugged them as tightly as I could.

My dad whispered, "You won't be here long, I promise."

And my mother began to cry and told me, "Get better. Please, get better."

As they left, I watched them walk further and further away until they crossed over to the hall with the steel door. I sat down with my dinner. I can't remember what it was as I was too distraught from the entire procedure I had gone through while I was being admitted. I simply stared at it for five minutes, struggling with Ana. Although I wanted to leave the hospital, Ana was still there and she was still fighting the system.

"You have to eat," the orderly told me.

"What if I can't?" I replied.

"If you don't eat now, you will have to get a feeding tube within the next day or two. Either you can eat on your own or we can force feed you that way." He stoically answered.
Ana crept into my mind and said, *you must avoid the feeding tube. The only way you will get out of this is by eating. As long as you are in here, you can't hide. He is watching you, so eat as slow as possible.*
I complied. I sat in front of my dinner, eating as slowly as possible over the next hour, until I could tell that the orderly was becoming tired of watching me.
"I think I'm done. I can't anymore," I told him, my voice shaking.
His response to that was, "Okay. I won't count this against you tonight but you must eat all of your food tomorrow or there will be repercussions." I nodded in agreement.
I was released into the living area where I sat down alone waiting for bedtime, which was at 10 pm for patients under 18. The staff called for bedtime preparation around 9:45. I washed my face while others waited for their turn. The mirror only allowed you to see your face and the windows around us were non-reflective so that we could not see our bodies. I saw some girls in the vanity room doing all they could to see how their bodies looked. My mission was to get out of there as soon as possible and go to bed. The faster I went to bed, the sooner a day would go by and the closer I'd be to going home.
I entered my room, and my two roommates were there. Their names were Chelsea and Mandy. Chelsea was the youngest of the three of us but had been there longer than most of the girls in the hospital... a total of 6 months. She was fifteen-years-old and suffered from bulimia nervosa. She was a cute blonde girl with a big smile. She had an outgoing personality, and I immediately liked her.
Mandy's bed was closest to mine. She towered over me in height. She was beautiful with long blonde hair and big beautiful brown eyes. She resembled a model at just sixteen, and in my opinion, had the perfect body. She was compassionate, kind and artistic. We connected right away. She had only been there for a week so far.

"So what's it really like here?" I asked as we sat on our hospital beds.
Chelsea was the first to answer my question by saying, "It sucks. It sucks really badly."
Mandy added on by saying, "There is no privacy. None. And it's strict."
"I can tell it's strict. What's up with those toilets?" I asked laughing.
"They like to look at our shit, I guess," Chelsea said, chuckling.
"So what do we do all day?" I asked.
"Well, it's really boring. We have a bunch of therapy groups and meal times. It gets really boring on the weekends. Literally nothing to do-- not even therapy," She responded as she yawned.
"Oh...yeah that does suck," I said.
"Can we turn out the lights? I'm tired!" Chelsea exclaimed. Mandy got up and turned off the lights and quickly hurried off into her bed.
"Oh, by the way, Syanne, don't be surprised by the nurses. They have to check on us every 30 minutes throughout the night. They also come in at 4 A.M for finger pricks," She added.
"Oh...okay thank you," I replied, confused. I had no idea that I would have to get my finger pricked at 4 A.M. It just made no sense to me as I had just had my blood drawn that day. I stayed up most of the night wondering what type of things I'd be going through. Any time I'd finally start drifting off to sleep, one of the nurses would peer in and loudly close the door...waking me up in the process. I became so tired that the noises no longer bothered me, and neither did my thoughts.
It can't be that bad... I told myself as I finally fell asleep. Reality did not really sink in until the next day.

Day One

I woke up in a panic the following morning as a nurse pushing a metal cart entered the room. I quickly sat up and looked around. This woke neither Chelsea nor Mandy up.
The nurse first stopped at Chelsea's bed, took her hand and I heard a loud click. It was the blood tester she had told me about. Chelsea did not even flinch when this was done. For being just 15, she was braver than I was. She then stopped at Mandy's bed. Mandy quietly sat up with her eyes half closed and extended her hand to her. Another loud click. Mandy made a face of discomfort but once it was finished, she laid back down and fell asleep. I then realized that it was my turn. I sat all the way up, extended my hand the way Mandy had done, and closed my eyes. Loud click, and it was over.
"Excuse me, ma'am, how often do I have to get my finger pricked? Once a week?" I asked.
She gave me a gentle smile and said, "No sweetheart, we have to do it every day for at least two weeks."
"Okay," I coldly responded, angry about the circumstances.
"Well, it's better than having to get your blood drawn through your vein," I thought to myself. The nurse smiled at me, and very rapidly left the room.
I was to wake up at 6:30 a.m., so there was no use in going back to sleep. I simply closed my eyes and began thinking about how I could be at home and going to school, but instead I was here, in a mental hospital wasting my life.
"I will be better. No more. I don't need Ana. I can't do this anymore," I told myself. Before I knew it, it was 6:30 a.m. I was the first one out of bed followed by Mandy. Chelsea stayed in bed as we left. Mandy was very kind to me, guiding me to where I needed to go and staying by my side.

The first stop was the nurses' station in the dormitory where we would receive hospital gowns that we had to change into for our morning weigh-ins. They were paper thin and barely covered anything. I theorized they did this to avoid any added weight. We all stood in a line, arms crossed, staring at the floor. As I glanced up, I noticed all of the emaciated women around me; some couldn't have weighed more than 60 something pounds. I had never seen anything like this before.

"And everyone thought I was sick. I'm perfectly fine compared to the rest of them," I thought.

It was my turn. They directed me to face away from the scale, and told me that my weight today would not count towards having any restrictions since it was my first day. I was relieved. I did not know what all of the restrictions were if you did not make weight, but I certainly had no desire in finding out.

I was then directed to one of two showers in the entire eating disorder unit. We all had to wait in line for our turn. If you made weight, you were able to shower for seven minutes. If you did not, you were not permitted to shower for three days. If you did not make weight two consecutive times, you would go six days without a shower and if it happened a third time you were finally allowed to shower for just two minutes. I don't understand how restricting someone of basic hygienic needs constitutes as therapy. The way I saw it, it was a form of punishment and torture.

One girl, Renee, had already gone six days without taking a shower. She was so frustrated with the situation that she went against their instructions and washed her hair in the sink. Renee was a small girl, the same age as me but looked at most to be 13-years-old. She may have been small but she was tough. I watched the nurses run to the vanity room to try to stop her from washing her hair.

"Are you serious? She's just washing her hair!" I turned and said to someone behind me in line.

"They don't give a fuck here. They are on a power trip. They don't care about us." they said, "you'll soon find out."

All of this felt unreal, like a movie that I was watching on Lifetime or something. There was just no way that what I was going through was real life. Before I knew it, it was my turn to shower. I quickly undressed, the 7-minute timer started as soon as you stepped foot through the shower room door. You had to be quick. I tried to wash myself as best I could and they began knocking on the door to alert me that five minutes passed. I had two minutes left. If I was not out and dressed in 7 minutes it would give them the right to come in and get me out of the shower while I was naked. Luckily, I made it out with just one minute left.

From there, we scrambled into the living area, patients trying to grab the first seat available. There weren't enough seats for all of us so if you didn't get a seat, you had to sit on the floor. We waited until it was time for us to take our medication, followed by breakfast. As I waited, the nurse called me back into one of her rooms. There was a line to her room, so I waited in silence, guessing that it was some sort of daily checkup. Once I got closer, I saw what was happening.

"It's time for you to get your blood drawn," she said.

"Wait, what? No, I had my blood drawn yesterday and I had my finger pricked this morning too." I said, confused.

 "Part of your evaluation and treatment is to have your blood drawn daily for 28 days and your finger pricked for the first two weeks, or as needed." She said sternly.

"No. I'm not okay with that. I already had it done yesterday; there's no point in doing it again." I turned around to leave but one of the orderlies had blocked the door.

"Syanne, please have a seat." She demanded.

 I crossed my arms, and sat down.

"Please uncross your arms," She asked.

"No. I don't have to," I responded. The nurse sighed and signaled for one of the orderlies to get Betty in the room. Betty came in and said, "What's wrong, Syanne?" She sounded concerned.

97

"They said I have to get my blood drawn again. I think it's a mistake, why would I have to get it done for 28 days straight?" I asked, completely baffled.
"They're correct, Syanne. It's what we have to do to keep you healthy. Please extend your arms." She requested.
I crossed my arms even tighter and quietly said *no*.
"We don't want to have to restrain you." She said.
 I ignored her, not thinking that they would actually put their hands on me. But I was wrong. Betty and the orderlies came closer to me and my first instinct was to push them away because I felt threatened. Betty grabbed my right arm, while an orderly grabbed my left arm. The nurse proceeded towards me to draw my blood. My heart began to race, and I thought, *"Is this really happening? This cannot be real."*
"Stop resisting or we could hurt you with this needle," she said, fighting to keep me still. I didn't have enough strength to continue to fight and very quickly lost the energy to try and push three adults off of me.
I cried as they proceeded to draw my blood, not because it hurt but because I felt out of control. Truly out of control of what was happening to my body. This was worse than the way that Ana had ever made me feel.
"See that wasn't so bad. If you do resist again, we will have to put you in restraints. Have a good breakfast!" She said with a smile.
 I quickly learned that she was not on my side. I walked out of the room, passing the line of girls that watched the scene I had caused, completely embarrassed with myself. This was just day one. I have to stay for at least six months. How will I survive?

Survival

When an animal becomes cornered or is caged, their survival instincts are released. They have two choices, fight or flight. I had now become the caged animal and for the first time ever, I felt what it was like to survive in difficult circumstances.

I did not have the option to flee, so the only choice I had left was to fight. I could no longer hear Ana, the only thing I cared about was getting out of this place.

Several weeks had passed and I had rapidly learned to adapt to my surroundings and environment. I knew every rule in the clinic and had been through a few of their punishments for not making weight. I had gotten into plenty of trouble for disruptions caused by myself and other hospitalized patients. The first time I did not make weight, I was shocked. I had been trying so hard to get well so that I could leave this horrible place. We were supposed to gain 0.2 kg a day or we would be put on restriction. I did not gain 0.2 kg that day and was punished, even though I had done nothing to stop the weight gain. I was eating all of my meals and was following all of the rules. My body had just hit a plateau after rapid weight gain. They instructed me not to take a shower for the next three days and my caloric intake would be increased as well. I was not permitted to call my parents, but did so anyway while another girl kept watch for me for nurses and orderlies. I called to let them know I had been put on restriction and if they called to let the girls know they were my parents and to discreetly get me on the phone. While I was in the middle of the phone conversation with my parents, one of the nurses behind the desk had spotted me and hung up the call.

"Um, excuse you...I was talking to my mom!" I yelled at her.
"It doesn't matter. We have orders here that say you are on restriction and cannot be on the phone." She snidely replied.
"That's cool, bitch. You're going to hate me later for that."
I muttered under my breath as I walked away.

I had started to become a very hateful person during my stay at the eating disorder clinic and in time no longer feared their punishments. After I had failed to make weight a second time, through no fault of my own, I once again was not permitted to shower for three more days. My hair was greasy and I smelled disgusting. I was still not able to talk to my parents and on top of it all, the clinic had put me on a treatment that they called "conservation therapy."

The way conservation therapy worked was by placing a patient in a chair, isolated from the rest of the patients in the clinic and instructing them not to move for the entire day, so about 12 hours. The only time they were allowed to move was for bathroom breaks or therapy sessions. In addition, the other patients were not allowed to talk to you; otherwise they'd get in trouble too. The way they explained conservation therapy to me was by saying that it was to "conserve calories by keeping me still."

 Out of all of the punishments that I had, this was the most difficult one. The first time I was placed in conservation therapy, I cried all day. I felt helpless because I could not call my parents and I had no one to help me. A nurse had approached me and tried to comfort me by telling me that this was necessary to save my life. The only words I could get out to her were, "leave me alone."

 I did not trust anyone in uniform in that building, no matter how kind they seemed.

As the weeks went by, I became stronger emotionally and physically. I no longer feared any of the threats or punishments they sent my way. I no longer even cared about having my blood drawn. You should have seen us– we looked like a bunch of heroin-addicted zombies, stumbling around the facility with our black and blue arms. The bruises covered more than 6 inches on each of my arms. Every time they stuck the needle in my skin it hurt more and more, but I reached such a high level of pain tolerance that I was able to mentally remove myself from the situation as it happened.

One day, after they had checked my blood, they did make a discovery. They found that I was going through re-feeding syndrome, which can be deadly. If you don't know, re-feeding syndrome is caused by severe starvation. Metabolic disturbances are caused as a result of the re-feeding process of starved people, which can easily cause a patient to die. I was put on a medication to help balance out my potassium in order to keep me alive.

If there is anything I am thankful for from the clinic, is the fact that they were able to find this and treat it and keep me alive. They also ordered that I have a bone scan. They had discovered that I was in the beginning stages of Osteoporosis, called Osteopenia, at just 16-years-old. Osteoporosis is a bone disease in which your bones become very brittle, and can easily be fractured. I was placed on medication for that condition as well.

While I am grateful that they did keep me alive, they also left me with mental trauma from the things I had seen in the clinic. I recall that one girl had become so depressed during her stay at the hospital that she stabbed herself in her vein with a pen. After that she could not be alone, not in the bathroom stall, and not while she slept. We could hear her weeping from her room as a nurse sat directly in front of her bed for the entire night.

What made it so difficult for these patients were the hospital punishments, their restrictions and their rules. We had to eat a "certain way". We could not have cereal the way the rest of the world has it. We had to eat the cereal separately and drink the milk separately. My best friend at the clinic and I ended up calling one of those nurses the "cereal Nazi" because she was especially particular about this. If anything, controlling the way we ate only contributed to our disorders. Many eating disorder sufferers strive to be in control and limiting their control in how they eat only makes their illness worse.

We were also not allowed to eat the same foods over and over again. They told us that doing this fed into our disorder because we were only allowing ourselves to have "safe foods." This wasn't true for me. The only reason I continued to get the biscuits over and over again was because they tasted wonderful. Although it was not true for me, this was the one rule that I did understand. I was guilty of having safe foods back home that included crackers, soymilk and cauliflower.

The next rule made no sense to me at all. They didn't like when we spent too much time with the same girls in the facility. They attempted to separate my best friend and I at the clinic because we were spending "too much time together". The nurses would rat us out to the doctors for singing and dancing around the hospital. We didn't exactly help the situation by talking back, and making songs about them...but it was what kept us from hurting ourselves in the circumstances that we faced.

Every time I would see my doctor, he would accuse me of trying to lose weight. I always told him that my goal was to leave the clinic and if I continued my behavior that I would never leave. He did not believe me. There was one day I was sitting in his office in a long-sleeved shirt and sweatpants and was anxiously shaking my leg. I was anxious because I did not like him.

He looked at me and said, "Are you wearing long sleeved and sweatpants because you think you're getting fat?"

My reply to that was, "I'm wearing long sleeves and sweatpants because it's comfortable and I have no one to impress in this building."

His response to this was with another question. "Are you shaking your leg because you're trying to burn off extra calories because you think you're fat?"

I stopped shaking my leg, looked him in the eyes and angrily responded with, "I'm shaking my leg because I'm bored and I don't really like you. I would like to leave your office now, please."

I was surprised that he did, in fact, allow me to leave without any repercussions. Or so I thought.

The next day I was put on restriction for not making weight for the first time in over a month. In addition, my doctor had called me in to let me know that I could no longer spend time with the group of girls I loved being with. Without them, I could not make it through this place alive. I objected and yelled at my doctor, asking why he felt that he had to do this. He told me that the nurses had said that we engaged in negative behavior together with the songs that we created about the facility, and about their doctors. He said he had no choice but to separate us.

"I want to go home," I told him.

"You're not well enough to go home." He answered.

"Okay. We'll see," I said as I walked out of his office.

Goodbye

Throughout my stay at the eating disorder clinic, I was sure to keep my parents up to date with what the hospital was doing-- whether on restriction or not. My hospital friends and I had ways to talk on the phone without directly talking on the phone. One way was by having our parents ask for another patient while we were on restriction and having them notify our parents of our progress and condition for us.

My last few days there I had called my dad in desperation while I was on restriction, begging him to come get me and telling him about all the things that were happening. After my 28 days were up, I was not supposed to continue to have my blood drawn. But for whatever reason, my doctor had ordered that the nurses continue to do it- even though I had already overcome re-feeding syndrome. My arms were completely bruised and hurt so bad that I could barely move them. I could not continue another day. My dad told me that he was coming up the next day to get me out of there.

"You can't come and see me dad, I'm on restriction. I'm not even supposed to be on the phone with you." I told him.

"I am your father. They cannot keep me from seeing my own daughter. I'm coming tomorrow," he confidently said to me.

"Okay, I'll see you tomorrow, I have to go. There is a nurse coming." And I quickly hung up the phone.

After I had hung up the phone, I let my friends know that I was leaving the clinic soon and that my dad was coming up the next day to let the facility know that he was discharging me from treatment. They told me that I would not be able to leave the next day because there was some sort of process that they had to go through in order to get me out that would take days.

Although I appreciated their insight, I also knew my dad and that he would do anything he could to get me out as soon as possible. My dad came to see me the next evening and they did try to tell him that I was not allowed to have visitors. I'm not sure how he did it, but they allowed him in to see me for about an hour. They regularly came in to "check on us." I think the real reason was so that they could try to catch parts of our conversation. By the end of his visit, he let me know that he was going to discuss with them the discharging process to get me out as soon as possible. From there, he told me that he loved me, hugged me and told me not to worry. He was getting me out.

I did not hear from him that evening but I did the next day. He informed me by phone that I would be able to leave in two days, and that the doctors had taken me off of restriction at his request. It was not easy, as he told me that they continuously told him that I was not healthy enough to leave. His response to them was that they would seek treatment for me elsewhere, in a place that did not treat their patients like criminals.

The next two days were the slowest of my time there. When I refused to get my blood drawn, they did not fight me to have it done. I think they were afraid of my father. I started skipping my therapy groups and spent my time in the living area drawing and writing.

My last night there was bittersweet. It was bittersweet because I was ecstatic to be ending my time at this horrendous clinic but it was bitter because I hated to leave my friends behind. I was getting out and they had no way of leaving. I felt tremendous guilt for leaving them behind. We weren't supposed to hug one another but I hugged each and every one of the patients. Not one of them cared of the repercussions that would follow for having physical contact with another patient, they loved me and did not know if they would ever see me again.

The truth is that I never did see them again-- but we did exchange numbers, and several of them had written me letters and drew me pictures. I promised that I would call to check on them when I got home.

I left the hospital and stepped outside for the first time in almost two months. I had forgotten what fresh air felt like, tasted like and smelled like. When I had gotten in the car, I had become nauseous since I had not ridden in a car in weeks. It did not bother me though, I was too busy taking in all of the sights I had taken for granted before. The trees looked greener and the sky looked bluer than ever before. Watching the sunset during the car ride was surreal. I could not believe how beautiful it was and how I had not noticed it before.

My dad and I stopped for ice cream and I embraced the taste, not worrying about Ana or what she had to tell me. When I got home, I felt peace. My room had never felt cozier and my bed felt more comfortable than ever. I decided to be brave and take a look in my full-length mirror for the first time in nearly two months. I was at a loss for words with how different I thought that I looked.

My cheeks were fuller, my breasts larger and my butt curvier. I looked more like a woman, and less like a little girl. I was no longer a size 00, or even a 0.

I went to bed smiling; feeling beautiful and grateful to be in the emotional state that I was in, back at home with my family where I belonged.

The Attempt

I wish that I could say that I lived happily ever after but that would be inaccurate. Within the next month I had not only relapsed, but had become very suicidal. I woke up many nights sweating, thinking that I was still in the eating disorder clinic. I never knew that my stay there would cause me to have nightmares for months to come. Returning to school was not easy. Everyone had found out that I had been hospitalized in a mental health facility and began calling me names like "fat", and "crazy." When I would walk the halls, I felt like everyone was staring at me. The torment from my peers had become so bad that I had to stop riding the bus.

I had turned back to Ana after I was continuously called fat. She slowly crept back into my mind, whispering to me that they were right. All the progress I had made was gone within weeks. Looking back, I realized that I never actually got better. Physically, I had drastically improved. But the hospital failed to treat the mental aspects of the illness, leaving me with no tools on how to cope with my emotions. You would think that surviving the clinic was enough to make me strong but what I struggled with was self-acceptance. I felt that the only way for me to validate myself was through the opinions others' had of me. I had thought that way since I was an 8-year-old girl. As sad as it is for me to reflect on this, it must be told.

I attempted to take my own life in the spring of 2009, two months after I was released from the clinic. I had once again dropped to the mid-80's in weight, my habits worse than ever before. My reason for doing this was out of desperation. I felt there was no way out from the bullying of my peers and I felt that I would never be rid of Ana. I was tired. Tired of suffering, and tired of trying to live.

I overdosed on anxiety medication that the clinic had prescribed to me, taking the rest of the medication-- which was at least a dozen pills. The good news is that I obviously made it. Once I had begun blacking out, I stormed out of my room and told my mother what I had done. Instead of calling an ambulance, she took me herself as she felt that she could get me there faster than the ambulance. I'm pretty sure she was right.

As I grew weaker on the car ride, I began to slur my words. I was in and out of consciousness, closing my eyes and waking up every few minutes. My mother spoke to me to keep me awake. Once I arrived, the hospital immediately took me back, and treated me with two doses of activated charcoal, which is used for severe poisoning, to counteract what I had the done. I'm not sure how long I spent lying there with heart machines attached to my skin, because everything blurred together. All I remember was being told that I had to be hospitalized again, this time for being suicidal. I thought that I was done with hospitalizations, done with fighting with mental illness and done with fighting for life. But God pulled me through for a reason.

Floor 5

Floor 5 was what patients called the psychiatric ward that I was admitted to. This hospital was much more relaxed and to be completely honest, was phenomenal. I was a PHP, which meant partial hospitalization patient. Since the hospital was only 20 minutes from my house, I was able to come home at night to sleep, only having to return from 7 a.m. - 6 p.m. every day.

Not only did I meet my best friend there of over 10 years, I also met quite a few interesting characters that I will never forget. One was named Sandra, and she was one of my favorite patients there. She was in her 50's and suffered from Schizophrenia. When I would arrive in the mornings, I would spend quite a bit of time with her until therapy started for the teenagers. She always took me on "make believe" shopping adventures with the help of fashion magazines that she kept. To her it was real and I enjoyed seeing her happy. She spent a lot of time talking about her son, whom she said never came to see her. Later I found out that she never had a son and had no children at all. In her mind, she did have a son and no one could make her think any different. The truth is that she was all alone in the world and the staff and patients of the facility were the only family she had. We all loved her.

There was another schizophrenic patient, but she was not happy like Sandra. This one was in her 40s and her name was Rose. In therapy, we would often hear her screaming and running in the halls. One day, she went into the bathroom and swore that there was blood all over the floor and walls. There was no consoling her as she screamed, "That's my blood all over the bathroom, oh my God, and that's my blood!" This was normal for her, and the nurses often had to sedate her to keep her from injuring herself and other patients.

Despite the many disruptions that occurred in the hospital halls, I never wanted to leave. The staff treated us all with compassion and love. There were no absurd rules. I was surprised when I found out that I could go to the bathroom whenever I wanted without asking. I didn't believe this, so I continued to ask until they grew so annoyed with me that they said, "This is not the eating disorder clinic! We do not stop you from having to pee. Please stop asking and just go."

I felt free. Completely free to say what I felt without judgment. In this hospital, I did receive the care that I needed. They spent time teaching us coping mechanism and used several different types of tools in teaching us. I only stayed for a month. I can't remember if my insurance would no longer cover my stay or if they felt I was well enough to return to normal. This was the only hospital I hated to leave, and cried when I left. I loved the staff and I loved the patients. Two staff members even cried when I left, pleading with me to use the tools that I had learned and to stay well.

I only wish that I could have promised them that I would.

Ana's Hand

I did not struggle with Ana for months and I had no suicidal thoughts. I was on new anti-depressants and felt wonderful. What's devastating is that when I returned to school, the torment began again as my peers learned of yet another hospitalization.
I tried my best to ignore it but despite my medication, years of therapy, and hospitalizations, I once again returned to the behavior that I had worked so hard to resist.
Ana was back in my mind and was more powerful than ever. She refused to let me go. I began to skip meals and eventually would go days without eating. My parents were at the end of their ropes and did not know how to help me anymore. The only way they could get me to eat was by threatening to admit me back to the eating disorder clinic that I hated. Looking back, I knew that they would never do that but they had to say something to get me to eat. Not only did I struggle with Ana, but I also struggled once again with suicidal thoughts. My parents had done their best to keep medications locked away from me by keeping them in a safe with a lock. But someone had forgotten to put a bottle of over the counter painkillers back in the safe and I took the advantage of the situation and impulsively took what was left in the bottle. It was not nearly enough to kill me but I ended up back in the hospital with activated charcoal to stop the overdose.
This time, my parents had decided not to admit me to a mental health facility. We all felt that they were not helping me and that I would continue to see my therapist two times a week. In place of hospitalization, the emergency room had me sign a contract that stated that I would not hurt myself. If I did not, they would be able to admit me to a psychiatric institution with no voluntary leave. I signed and agreed not to do it again.
This is one thing that I am proud to say that I never, ever did again.

However, I did continue to struggle with Anorexia for three more years, reaching my lowest weight of 79 pounds at the age of 19. I was in and out of the emergency room, my doctor warning me of impending heart failure at any time. I had been diagnosed with osteoporosis. I did not go to college, I did not have a job and I did not have any friends. I spent most of days laying down, praying to God that he would take me Home so that my suffering would end. But He had bigger plans for me

Life Without Ana

Recovery was not easy. Recovery was hard work. It is perhaps the most difficult thing that I have ever had to do. It required faith, continuous support from those around me, as well as professional help. My secret to reaching complete recovery from Anorexia Nervosa was actively helping others'. I became very active in the community and often volunteered with different organizations including The BULLY Project. Volunteering gave me purpose and I knew that in order to help others' I had to be well myself. I could not serve as a role model if I was slowly killing myself. I've learned how to live without Ana. I've learned how to enjoy food as a necessity to keep me alive. When I say I now enjoy food, I mean it. In fact, food makes me happy. I have not relapsed in 7 years nor is there any indication that I would ever go back to Ana. In these 7 years that I have been free from Ana I have entered several beauty pageants and most notably held the title of Miss Maryland 2015 for the Miss World Organization. The highlight of my reign was when I placed in the Top 12 at Miss World America. I am sure this seems contradictory to my recovery, as critics believe that beauty pageants encourage unrealistic beauty standards. I found quite the opposite. It encouraged me to become physically healthy and fit because the purpose of a pageant title is to be a role model. To be a role model means to be healthy.

However, I wish that I could say that I was healthy mentally as well. Although I overcame my battle with Anorexia Nervosa, I still struggled with mental health issues in 2016 and 2017, particularly Borderline Personality Disorder. To this day I still experience mental anguish but I've learned healthy coping skills when it gets tough. I made a vow to never return to Ana because my life depends on staying away from her. When I begin to fall down into a pit of depression, what I've found to be my saving grace is ASKING FOR HELP. This is not as easy as it sounds. I understand that asking for help can make you feel like you are burdening others'. But I promise you are not. You are important to everyone around you and they need you to be around. These are things I don't just speak to other people. I also speak it to myself. It is essential for my survival.

It would be extremely unrealistic to say that my life is perfect now. I still see mental health professionals. Mental illness is like any other chronic condition; it takes continuous support to reach remission. But first you must take the steps to getting help.

Get Help

There were multiple problems that had occurred in my life that possibly triggered my eating disorder, such as moving from the U.S Virgin Islands to California and being bullied. As a child, I struggled to understand how to manage the changes that were happening around me and the abuse that I was receiving from my peers. I couldn't understand what was happening or how to deal with what was happening without the help from counselors, my family, nor those around me knew how to solve my problems. In essence, I was alone to act out my sins without the presence of God in my life. Being human means that sin is all around us and responding to sinful acts is the easiest way to cope with stress and pain. It may be the easiest way but it is incredibly dangerous not just to the physical body, but also to the soul. I had responded to the stress in my life with sin by manipulation, deception, and ultimately, worshipping the sin that I had come to know as "Ana."

Instead of turning to God or mental health professionals, I idolized the women I had found through social media sites for their loyalty to their eating disorders. It wasn't until I became an adult that I learned that love and happiness is found through Christ, and not by temptations to sin.

To overcome Anorexia Nervosa (or any eating disorder), we must recognize what leads us to sin through this behavior. Was there a stressful situation in the sufferer's life? Family conflicts? Was there a major loss in the sufferer's life? Or a traumatic event?

These are examples of events in the lives of sufferers that need to be explored to get to the root of the problem with the aid of mental health professionals and medical experts.

I highly recommend seeking aid from the **National Eating Disorder Association (NEDA)**, a non-profit organization in the United States that advocates for individuals and families battling eating disorders. Their website at <nationaleatingdisorders.org> has an incredible amount of resources that saves lives. It offers a network for parents, family and friends of sufferers of eating disorders that highlight ways to support those with eating disorders. This organization is the resource that I refer families and sufferers to.

In addition, NEDA also has a toll-free, confidential Helpline available Monday-Thursday (9A.M-9P.M) and Friday (9 A.M-5PM EST). And if you don't feel comfortable talking on the phone, the Helpline is also available online through their website.

Bulimia.com, not just for Bulimia but also for any eating disorder, is a resource that provides information and treatment center resources— connecting you directly with eating disorder treatment centers that fit your needs.

From a Christian perspective, I recommend also seeking the help of a Biblical Counselor, perhaps using the help of your church or pastor. A team must be assembled with God, with doctors, mental health experts, friends and family for the sufferer to receive deliverance from the hands of an eating disorder.

Other Resources:
Center4ed.org
Recoveryspark.com
ANAD.org

Acknowledgments

I want to give my thanks to: Joseph Bloom, my wonderful fiancé, for his support in encouraging me to finish this book. I love you always. I want to thank mother and father for doing everything in their power to save me from this horrible illness and for supporting me throughout the process of publishing this book. My friends for being my cheerleaders throughout the rollercoaster process of getting this book to the public. I love you all.

Manufactured by Amazon.ca
Bolton, ON